# The Great Truth:

# God Is Real

By

Christmas Blizzard

# Table of Contents

# DEDICATION

I dedicate this book to my mom, Faith Blizzard. She was the greatest friend and supporter I have ever had in my life. Mom, I miss you every day. I hope they allow books in heaven.

Chris Blizzard

# ACKNOWLEDGMENTS

This book would not be possible without God. As a matter of fact, I would have died back in 1987 and I would be a statistic you never even heard of, let alone someone who wrote the book you're reading.

# INTRODUCTION

Other than the Bible, have you read a good Christian book lately? I haven't. At least I couldn't find one during the *week* I spent at the Christian bookstore *one morning*. Not only could I not find one I liked, but I couldn't find one like the one I felt compelled to write.

Not to be deterred by my bestseller disappointment, I spent the afternoon researching divine intervention books with a librarian. As usual, I needed professional help. But to my surprise, she couldn't find any books like mine, either. Between the bookstore and the library, my day of research brought me to two basic conclusions: One, Christian books suck. And two, they're boring.

First, it's as if they're all trying to win Christian Book of the Month Club awards by proving how well they adhere to the Bible. I saw book after book laden with verses that nicely fit whatever they said to show how biblically correct they were. I do not doubt that when Christian books are released; various biblical groups check for things that go against Scripture. If they find them, the book gets swept aside as scriptural rubbish. No prize for you!

Secondly, the books I found about divine interventions all involved hearing voices or seeing visions. They didn't involve anything physically happening. I'm not discounting those experiences, but come on, hearing voices? If I told you I was hearing voices and seeing things, would you want to read a book I wrote about God? Well, let me say that I have never heard a voice or seen a vision (sober), and that is not what this book is about.

My views on God come from the Bible and are confirmed by my personal experiences with God rather than Scripture. So sometimes, I may match the Bible, and sometimes, I may not. I'm not worried about that. I hope you're not either; otherwise, this book will likely disappoint you.

This is a different book about God. I say, God, as in God the father of Jesus Christ- my personal Lord and Savior. And I say 'different' because although I'm a Christian, this is not a book about Jesus Christ. I am not qualified to teach you anything about being a better Christian. Honest to God, I'm not. That is neither my job nor the intention of this book. If that's what you need (And really who doesn't?) then by all means, go to church. I do. Sometimes. The purpose of this book is twofold: It is to help give you reaffirmation that God is real and to help you see God working in your own life, by showing you examples of how He has worked in mine. That's it.

UPDATE: The preceding is how I started this book originally. I published it on my own through Createspace. Now, it's 2024. I last touched this book in 2015. My life has changed a lot since then. Many things have happened that will undoubtedly change this book as I go back through it before republishing.

In 2017, for instance, I graduated from Arizona State University with my BA in Theatre. During this time, I was a caretaker for an elderly lady I lived with for 7 years. It was a dark time in my life that God carried me through, not unscathed. I will try to stick to the details that are consequential to you. I may skip any references to that as it all happened after this book ends. The biggest thing that applies here is the changing of my book title. Originally, this book was called, Seeing God: A True Account of Divine Interventions. Since originally titling and publishing this book, I became fascinated with how the universe began. At one point I immersed myself in YouTube videos on every scientific subject from Einstein's theory of general relativity to The Big Bang Theory, to quantum mechanics, and so on.

I began listening to people like Neal deGrass Tyson and the late Dr. Stephen Hawking. I also took an interest in UFOs. I've heard several people say that discovering aliens from outer space would be the greatest discovery of humankind. Is that true? What about learning God exists? To me, that would be the greatest discovery for humankind. Or alien-kind for that matter. After all, if space aliens exist, God created them too. What could be a greater, more important discovery than learning God exists?

Since learning about The Great Pyramid in Egypt as a child, I have been fascinated by the question, how were they constructed? How did people move blocks of stone weighing hundreds of tons? How did they cut them with primitive tools and make them turn out perfectly? When I first heard about them in grade school, scientists didn't know. I grew up thinking at some point, scientists will figure it out and all will be explained to me. That day never came. The prevailing theory seems to be that they were created by space aliens. Hmm? As strange as that theory may be, I haven't ruled it out.

$E = MC^2$. That seems to be true; unless a black hole is involved. Once you get past the event horizon (The point near a black hole where there is no return and even light can escape being pulled in), that scientific law breaks down and is no longer true. Mr. Tyson and Dr. Hawking are and were devoted atheists. Mr. Tyson even believes Man's activity is changing the weather (Man-caused climate change). What is truth? How did the universe begin? Was it a Big Bang that came out of nothing and formed everything? When asked what existed before the Big Bang, Dr, Hawking and Mr. Tyson said the same thing, "What's south of the South Pole?" They attempt to answer a question with an unanswerable question- implying no one could know what existed before the Big Bang. That is idiotic. I contend neither of those two could be that stupid. The answer to the question of, *what existed before the Big Bang*, is so simple a 5th grader could answer it. *Whatever went*

5

*bang!* That's the answer. But neither of them will admit that. They're so dedicated to proving God doesn't exist, that they purposely mislead the population into believing a nonsensical argument.

Stolmaic. That is the previously accepted scientific belief that the earth is at the center of the universe and everything revolves around it. Of course, that was proven false long ago. However, some people still believe that and the Earth is flat. Currently, is man changing the weather? Do space aliens exist? Have they visited Earth in the past? Did they build the pyramids? Are they with us now? What is true?

Those questions and many others led me to change the name of my book from Seeing God: A True Account of Divine Interventions, to The Great Truth: God is Real. Hopefully, my book will appeal to the religious community, but I would also like to appeal to the scientific community. Mr. Tyson has hold of many young minds and is gleefully leading them to hell. I hope, through humility, that I can help their followers discover that God is real.

My promise before we begin: At the end of this book I will reveal what I believe are the two most important laws in the universe. I will tell you what they are and explain how I came to that realization.

# Chapter 1 Millbrook Road 0 to 7

## In the beginning, there was a childhood

Growing up in the country, I knew everything I wanted for Christmas within a week of the new JCPenney catalog arriving. I could recite the page number and corresponding item number of the exact cowboy cap gun, pistol, and rifle set (cheesy badge and handcuffs go in the trash), by heart. So could Mom. I made sure of that.

I remember Mom and Dad yelling at each other once; and hugging once. I have no memories of them talking. I'm sure they did, but they must not have done it around me. That pretty much sums up my early memories of them together.

My dad, Liston (God rest his soul), worked a lot. When he was at home, he was either tired or in his woodshop. He built everything from the house we lived in, into our china cabinets and the model airplanes that were suspended from the ceiling in the breezeway. Later in life, he made several real airplanes with collapsible wings. He truly had carpenter's hands. He was a gentle, hard-working man.

Faith (God rest her soul), with eight kids, was a stay-at-home mom. I could almost always talk her into buying Coney Island hot dogs when I would tag along on her Avon route. I spent a lot of time with Mom. When I wasn't under her wing (which she instinctively put across my chest to keep me from eating the Rambler's dash when she touched the brakes), I was at the mercy of my siblings.

Our family has always been divided into two groups- the older ones and the younger ones. Me, Matt, and Aaron Ray were *Younger*. Andy, Nick, Tammy, Tony, and John were *Older*.

7

John is my oldest brother- from my dad's first marriage. He was on his own and married as far back as my memory goes.

Tony, who is a few years younger than John, came from my mom's first marriage. If memory serves, he lived at home until *The Divorce*. I have limited, but pleasant memories of both John and Tony from that time.

Tammy, on the other hand, a couple of years younger than Tony, was the one you had to watch out for. She went through a phase in high school where she burned candles and prayed to the dark underworld; usually to bring evil curses on one of us, youngers.

Next was Nick, then Andy. Like most Blizzards, they were trouble on their own, but with Tammy's morbid direction, they took the responsibility to gather either Matt or Aaron- as human sacrifices, very seriously. Thankfully, since I was usually less than five years old, they mostly left me alone. But I watched Matt and Aaron Ray get absolutely tormented; while I hid, grateful it wasn't me.

One day they used a dog chain to tie Matt to a wagon in the basement. I remember watching as crickets were dropped into his mouth. When he clamped his lips shut, he was punched. When he'd open his mouth to howl; in went another bug. At one point, someone even fed him a praying mantis. Don't get me wrong; I wasn't exactly the scared little kid hiding in the corner. Well, not once they got him tied down, anyway. Then I was punching him too. It was funny; everyone had to open their mouth to scream.

That bit of childhood- like so many things, stick around clear as yesterday, like when I shot my brother, *A*aron. I was probably six or seven years old at the time. I believe it was during the first year my parents were divorced. During this time, Dad was married to a new wife. They shared a mobile home across town and a marriage that lasted all of one year. We kids (except married John) still lived in our 'birth' house on Millbrook Rd.

One day, we, brothers were hanging out in the front yard, being kids. Several of them were shooting their pump BB guns while I was trying out my brand-new lever-action. I don't remember who bought it for me, but it must have been Mom. It was brand new. I remember that. It wasn't the fancy one with the wooden stock, but it was OK. The BBs went kind of slow so when shooting the mailbox from the porch, the BBs lost enough elevation that I had to aim about six inches high to compensate.

As it 'tinged' off the mailbox, I wondered how much it would hurt to get shot by one. Surly, a BB going so slow you could see it fly wouldn't hurt, much, right? Well, there was one to find out. And he was sitting in the grass; looking like a target.

Since Ray was about half the distance to the mailbox, I only had to aim a couple of inches above his arm to hit True. I figured he would probably think a bee stung him and look around, confused. Then maybe go back to reading his book. I wondered how long that would last before he finally figured out it wasn't really a bee or a horsefly, but gosh darn it- he was being shot by his own brother. Well, I was about to find out. And as it turned out, he figured it out after the first shot.

"YOW!" He howled... and looked straight at me. Then he started jumping around and yelling all sorts of things I can't remember; or publish, even if I could. Talk about a drama queen. It was not the reaction I envisioned. Finally, he stopped dancing, looked at me with death in his eyes, and clenched his fists.

"I'm sorry." I accurately stated, tossed the gun, and took off. I ran down Millbrook Road to save my life. I looked back to see four or five of my brothers chasing me, with Ray in the lead. By the time I reached the asphalt of Mission Road nearly half a mile later; everyone, shooting victim included, had given up trying to catch me. Mom was screaming and smashing my gun across the porch, plastic rifle stock flying everywhere. I remember thinking that I could make another gunstock with Dad's woodworking tools as long as she didn't damage the barrel. Then she wedged the gun between two bricks and bent the barrel in half. Well, so much for that idea.

As I walked down Mission Rd, good old brother John happened by on his way home from work. He picked up his lost little brother and took me out for pizza and root beer. He called home to say I was with him. Then he calmed me down with good brotherly conversation and brought me back home.

Other than being fun to plink Ray again, I offer that little sidetrack for two reasons. First, I did it to show how my decision-making abilities have never been quite right. I mean, how could I think he wouldn't know he just got shot by the kid standing fifteen feet away with a BB gun pointed at him? Second, just like punching poor Matt in the wagon, why would I do those things to anyone, much less family? I simply don't know.

To summarize that chapter of my life, my zero to seven years weren't perfect. Is anyone's? After Dad's third marriage failed, he moved back home. The Older ones stayed with him on Millbrook, while we Younger ones were sent to live with Mom in town. Honestly, I got along with my mom. I loved my dad, but he was mostly a stranger to me. The Olders had a closer bond with him. I was OK with getting away from them, anyway. Sometimes they scared the crap out of me.

# Chapter 2 West Side Story

## The Cracker Box on Maxwell Street

I have never known (nor cared) about the details of my parent's divorce, but it seems to me that Mom got screwed. Basically, Dad kept his house in the country (He built it, why shouldn't he?) and we Youngers went with Mom to live in a one-bedroom dump on the bad side of town. Don't get me wrong; we didn't have gangs or crack houses. We weren't living in a ghetto, but there were a lot of unsupervised kids, like me. Homes in my neighborhood weren't as nice as the others around town. Some (if not most) of my friends lived in what can best be described as shacks. And since I was familiar with the worst in town, I can confidently say that during the mid-1970s, Mom, Matt, Aaron Ray, and I literally lived in one of the worst piece of shacks in Mt. Pleasant, Michigan. My little sister, Sharon, was born a couple of years after we moved there, but her father sadly died when she was a baby. That made five of us live in a 400 sq. ft. crate; we aptly called The Cracker Box On Maxwell Street.

After we moved to the Cracker Box, Mom basically turned me loose on the world. The self-destructive side of me was always there, growing up in the country, and only came out for the occasional BB gun plink or torture session. But once I was left to my own peril... well, let's just say I periled. I made one bad choice after the next. When things turned out bad, I got mad. When I got mad, things got bad. That made me madder... and things got *worse*.

I think Mom did her best to deal with my troublemaking ways, but she was simply overwhelmed, emotionally and financially, by the divorce. She couldn't control me. No one could. From time to time one of my brothers would try to discipline me, but they did so at the risk of great peril. It was not unlike me to attack them with a baseball bat, a knife (which I always carried), or any other instrument of death, which happened to be close at hand. *Just try me!*

One day Matt tried to keep me at home because I took the day off from school to nurse a sprained ankle. He was home with the honest-to-goodness flu and didn't want me going off to enjoy myself on a school day. He actually told me that I couldn't leave the house. Naturally, I picked up the wooden, purple softball bat.

"I dare you," was the last thing he said.

 I threw it across the very small living room with everything I had. I remember it as if it were yesterday. The bat spun end over end (in slow-motion as I recall) until the fat end connected with his forehead with a solid, "Thwap!"

Ever since we were kids, Matt was tough. He could dish it out and he could take it. But he was no match for the purple bat. He went down hard and fast. I high-tailed it out the back door before he could wake up and exact his revenge. I hobbled down the alley- as fast as my bum leg would take me- and snuck into Potsa's house (they were in school) and stayed there until Matt woke up and calmed down.

## Potsa, Shannon, and Sunnyside Park

Potsa and Shannon were brothers that I met when we moved to Maxwell Street. Potsa was close to me in age and his brother was about a year younger than him. So basically we were all the same age. They were half African-American and half Native-American; or as we used to say, half black and half Indian. I only mention that because it raised me colorblind. They were my best friends. That's all I knew. As a matter of fact, we are still good friends to this day.

There was an empty field across from the Cracker Box. In the middle of that was Sunnyside Park. Sunnyside is where the bad kids hang out. Sure, there was a set of swings, a slide; sand, and climbing things (Like any normal park) but there was also a gazebo. That's where we delinquents could get out of the weather to pass *cigs*, doobies, and even the occasional bottle of alcohol (beer, wine, whiskey... whatever someone could swipe). Never worried about getting caught; parents didn't bring their kids to Sunnyside; that place was for hoodlums.

Which made it perfect for my friends and me. It's where; by the end of my first week in town (at the ripe age of seven) I became an everyday cigarette smoker. I didn't start smoking weed until I was nine.

I found the weed escape one night with Potsa, Shannon, and their babysitter. They credited the sitter for getting them high their first time, but their mom used to let them puff joints to show off in front of her friends. I'm not sure exactly what she was showing off, but I'm pretty sure it wasn't her parenting skills.

Anyway, once we found out how much we liked smoking pot, all we had to do was figure out where their mom kept her stash; then we had it within easy reach. Well, until she noticed buds missing and re-hid her bag. Then, it was just a matter of finding her new hiding place; which was usually another shirt pocket in the same closet.

## Five finger discounting

Cigarettes were another matter. Not only would their mom have noticed stolen cigs, but she smoked those thin, dark ones that were three feet long. Not cool. Besides, we needed more than an occasional smoke pilferage to feed our nicotine monkeys. And on the budget of three poor kids under age ten, we needed serious five-finger discounts, all over the town.

The thing about that discount; I was a lousy shoplifter. Quite simply, I sucked at stealing. Well, getting caught every month or so is a gauge of shoplifting proficiency. My biggest problem was, I was an open book. I've always been an easy read. Any cashier could tell I was up to no good.

One day Potsa and I were in Ben Franklin's Five and Dime to do some discounting in the toy department. A cashier walked past while we were (very nonchalantly) making idle chitchat. You know, just two well-mannered kids. She leered at me and said, "May I help you boys?"

"No thank you, ma'am," I said. "We're just here to do a little shoplifting." Pause. "I mean shopping!" Potsa's eyes got huge. We both started laughing and walked out, *bootyless*. Yeah, I am an easy read. Or as Potsa said, "Blizzard, you're an idiot." Both seem fitting enough.

Even back in the 70s- when getting caught shoplifting was little more than a ride home from the cops; eventually, even they got tired of doing that. After my sixth or seventh time riding home in the back of a cop car, Mom and I were given a court date.

## Long Arm of the Law

Judge Personality (Not his real name) put me on probation. Before knocking his gavel, he said, "Mr. Blizzard, the next time you come to see me, bring your toothbrush." That comment made no sense whatsoever. I nodded and thanked him.

# Movin' On Up

It was around this time that Mom moved us from Maxwell Street to Arnold Street. It was a bigger house on the better side of town. It was still tiny, with four tiny bedrooms, but it was certainly a lot better than a tiny house with one tiny bedroom. I wasn't there very long though.

Despite being in a nicer home in a better neighborhood, while psychologists tried to figure me out, I kept stealing and getting in trouble. I even broke into the Island Park Hothouse. Then, for reasons I can't remember or imagine, I reported it to the cops. Yeah, I'm not very bright. I ended up right back in front of the judge.

# About that toothbrush...

"Mr. Blizzard. Did you bring your toothbrush?" he began.

"My teeth are clean," I said... even though I'm sure they weren't. How was he going to know from the bench?

"Do you remember the last time you were in front of me I told you, the next time you come to see me, bring your toothbrush?"

I remembered him saying something about a toothbrush, but I honestly thought he cared about my teeth. I didn't know why. I figured it was a parenting thing. He sure gave soothing talks whenever I saw him... so I knew he cared.

As I thought over the toothbrush question, he went on without an answer. "Go home and pack your toothbrush. Tomorrow someone will

15

drive you up to Eagle Boy's Village. The Village will send you back to your mother when you learn how to behave yourself blah, blah, blah." Gavel.

# Chapter 3 It Took a Village

Leave it to Mom to find the silver lining. The morning following my court hearing she said, "I hear they have horses and go roller skating at Eagle Boy's, Chris. I bet you end up having a great time. I packed your clothes."

"Yeah, I can see that," I said, looking at four brown grocery bags stuffed with my clothes. Paper bags were our luggage in those days. Suitcases were for rich people and angry gorillas. My next memory is riding in a car with someone forgettable the court had sent to pick me up. We arrived at Eagle Boy's Village two hours later. For some reason, I remember the date, December 7, 1976, Tuesday... a day that shall live in my infamy.

Eagle Boy's Village had seven or eight houses scattered over thousands of wooded acres in northern Michigan. Each house held ten kids with a husband and wife team that lived with them and ran the home. When I arrived, all the houses were full so I was sent to live at the private home of the Hanley Family. They were in charge of the Village's overall operation and ran the horse farm located across the road from their home.

Suddenly, I had to wake up at five every morning to feed horses and shovel crap before school. I didn't mind though. It was my first time around horses and I quickly fell in love with them. It was also when I learned what happens to a horse when it has a bad leg.

Kerm Hanley (the old man) was loading his 30-30 Winchester in the barn one night and heard me walk in. "Hey, Chris, come on over here," he said. "I want to show you something." He knelt and stroked the mane of a black horse that was lying down. He explained that the horse

17

needed to be 'put down' because it had a broken leg that would never heal right.

"Why don't you let her keep lying down and resting? Maybe it will get better with more time," I offered.

Me building an epic snow fort while home for the weekend from Eagle Boy's- winter 1976/77. Thanks for taking the picture, Mom.

"That's the problem. She's been lying down for three days now. Horses almost never lie down. If she would stand on it, I'd give her more time. Right now, she's just suffering. Putting her out of her misery is the right thing to do. Sometimes you have to do unpleasant things in life. That's just part of being a man. Help me walk her up on the trailer."

He had a trailer backed up to the barn and I could see he meant to 'put her down' in that so she would be loaded for transport- to wherever they take beautiful, black dead horses. "Do you want to watch?" he asked. "I warn you though, it's not pretty."

"I'll pass on that," I said, not having to think it over. We said our goodnights and I walked out of the barn. A little while later I heard a gunshot. To this day, I'm glad I skipped that manhood experience.

Me during a recent return. It is now Eagle Village and I am a bit older, but they still remembered me (Of course) and welcomed me back with great affection. I even got to speak with Kerm. It was a good visit.

I ended up staying with Kerm and his family for nearly a week until a spot opened up in one of the houses. Then I was sent to live with nine other delinquents and two 'house parents'.

Although growing up, Mom took my brothers and me to church, Eagle Boy's Village is where I became a Christian. Looking back, it's also where I saw God for the first time. No, I don't mean I physically saw Him. I saw His blessings. One day, while I was riding in one of the

19

vans full of kids (the troop carrying type, all bench seats) I was thinking to myself; as much as it sucks to be here, this is good for me. This is what I need. That's why God has me here. I remember feeling God's presence in the van that day. I felt like He was watching over me and that I was EXACTLY where God wanted me.

That was not only the first time I saw God, but also I think God saw me seeing Him that day. It wasn't an Intermonial by definition, since nothing physically happened, but that memory, after all these years, is still vivid. I even remember what road we were on; we were passing the Hanley farm.

# Front Door/Back Door

When I first got to Eagle Boy's, I was told there were only two ways out of the Village, the front door or the back door. If you went out the front door that meant whatever was wrong with you was fixed and you're ready to be returned to society. If you went out the back door that meant whatever was wrong with you was so severe; you needed to be locked up. That meant Boy's Training School (BTS) and bars. Eagle Boy's didn't have bars. You could run away any time you wanted. You simply had to get out of bed in the middle of the night and go for a walk. And as soon as you were arrested (which everyone was eventually... we were only teenagers for crying out loud. Well, most of them were. I was nine) it meant BTS... which was still leaving out the back door... just with a long walk.

# Afro Joe and The Side Door

I wasn't stupid enough to go the back route. But I wasn't smart enough to put on a good face long enough to get out the front door either. The management knew about my anger issues. I wasn't a terrible kid. I just had a temper; combined with a propensity for screwing up. I was there so long I became somewhat of an institution. Everyone knew me. I had stayed in five of the seven different houses by the time the *Overseers* decided it was time for me to move on.

To help them decide whether to send me home or to BTS, they told me I was going to be released when my mother came the following weekend- even though they had no intention of sending me home. They just wanted to see how I would react to the bad news. I was all set to go home with her and spent the week counting my final days of incarceration. I even walked around the house singing songs about it.

Then Saturday came. Mom showed up with two paper grocery bags full of clothes. I ran out to tell her she was confused. "Put the clothes back in the car. I'm going home with you today! You're here to pick me up, not bring me more clothes. I have my stuff packed."

"You must have misunderstood," she explained. "You're staying here for at least a few more months."

I ran back inside and demanded to know what was going on. It turns out Mom was right. I wasn't going anywhere. The management was *very sorry for any confusion*. Needless to say, I was on the verge of exploding, which is exactly what they expected me to do. I grabbed the bags of clothes Mom had brought and threw them against my bedroom wall. Suddenly, I felt the test on me. I knew the staff were all keenly attuned to how I would handle the bad news. Instead of giving them the temper tantrum they expected, however, I lay down and cried

21

myself to sleep.

A few days later, Afro Joe showed up- unannounced- during our nightly 'rap' session. A rap session is where we sat in a circle while everyone vented whatever concerns they had in their young, delinquent lives. "Blizzard, Blizzard, Blizzard. What are we going to do with you?" Joe asked. "Three to six months; that's how long most people are here. They get better and we send them home through the front door or they get worse and we send them to BTS through the back door... but they leave. Not you. Not Blizzard. You just stick around. You're not getting any better so we can't send you out the front door. And you're not getting any worse so we don't feel it's right to send you out the back door. What are we going to do?"

"You have to let me go when I turn eighteen don't you?" I asked, doing rough math, subtracting fifth grade from twelfth.

"Blizzard, Blizzard, Blizzard," he repeated. "You're forcing me to break the rule I have preached to every kid who's ever been through here, yourself included. There are two doors out of Eagle Boy's. That's all there's ever been. But I'm going to make a new one... just to get rid of you. And just this once!" He emphasized, eyeing the group. "Blizzard, you're going out the side door. I didn't even know we had one."

"Neither did I," I said, "but it sounds like you got that installed just in time. When do I leave?"

"I'll drive you home this weekend. I won't ask your mother to make the drive two weekends in a row."

That confirmed my "test" theory about Mom's previous visit with the armload of clothes when I was anticipating my release. I know that if I had lost my temper and thrown a fit, I would have been shipped to

BTS. Instead, I wore them out. I was going home out the newly created Side Door.

Two days after his side door speech, Afro-Joe drove me home. I call him Afro Joe for two reasons. One, I can't remember his real name; two, I can't forget his Afro. I'm talking about 1978 in all its glory. He looked like a chia pet on steroids. When he drove me home in his Datsun, the roof flattened on top, causing it to grow even larger on the sides. When he turned to face me, he looked like a hair-football with a face in the center. Of course, I remember having platform shoes, bell-bottom jeans, and three-inch wide watchbands- so I'm not without my seventies sins- but that Afro was huge! Absolutely magnificent.

Sorry for getting sidetracked. I will occasionally splash on some extra stuff; like exiting out the side door from Eagle Boy's. I don't know how relevant it is to Seeing God, but it sure was fun to see Afro Joe again.

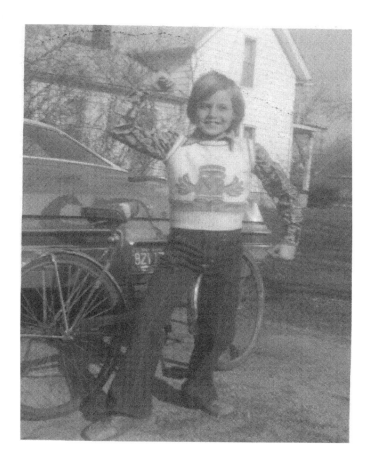

Home from Eagles Boy's. I had to include this picture. What's not to love?

# Chapter 4 Blanca

When Eagle Boy released me back into society (and the fifth grade), Mom let me get my own dog. Growing up, we always had lots of dogs. One day, at our house on Millbrook, I counted nine of them in our breezeway. Nine! Mom assigned me one when I was around four or five that I named Little Red. God love that dog, he was retarded. Not mentally challenged, mind you, but full-blown retarded. Even as an oblivious toddler, I could see that. Mom got rid of him and I didn't mind. When I got back from The Village, however, she let me pick my own dog. That's when I got Blanca.

A friend had a batch of puppies and I begged my mom to let me have one. "Bring it home so I can take a look at it," she told me. With that bit of approval, I lit a smoke and walked to my friend, Pat's, house. Since the puppies were only six weeks old, they were still suckling at their mom and he had the full litter. After digging through a squirming pile of *sucklers* I found a black one at the bottom of the pile, half the size of its brothers and sisters. "I'll take this one!" I told Pat, picking up my dog and kissing her.

"That's the runt," he gasped. "They get picked last."

"Maybe they normally do," I told him, "but today is different. Today the smallest one gets picked first." With that said, I slipped her into my shirt pocket and walked home to show Mom. I wasn't worried about her looking at it and sending me back. Mom was always a sucker for dogs.

"Isn't she precious?" Mom cooed, as Blanca peered out of my shirt pocket. "What are you gonna name her?"

Sixth grade was the beginning of my love affair with nature. I had just finished reading a story about a fabled livestock-killing wolf, the farmers called, Lobo. His mate was a white wolf named Blanca. If my dog had been a male, I would have named him Lobo. Instead, she was a female. So I named her after Lobo's mate. "Her name will be Blanca," I said.

"That means 'white' in Spanish," she said. "That dog is black."

"I know both of those things Mom. Blanca is just a cool name."

"I agree," she said and hugged me. "Take good care of Blanca. She's your responsibility."

Of course, I could always rely on Mom to take care of her, but from fifth grade through twelfth, that dog and I were inseparable. Except for school, I took her pretty much everywhere I went. I trained her to stay on my right side so when I rode my bike through town, so as long as I went with traffic, she was able to run along beside me by the sidewalk, out of the road. Mind you, this was back in the day of stray dogs and little (if any) leash laws. From time to time, someone would leer at me because my dog was loose, but no one ever said anything. Frankly, I wouldn't have cared even if they had. Blanca was my best friend. At home, Mom kept her in a dog pen or tied up, but with me she was free.

# Flipper

Now that I lived on the East side instead of the West side, Island Park was six blocks of middle-class homes away. It was much better than living across from Sunnyside Park. Island Park had a public swimming pool, picnic areas, and an ice-skating rink. It also had that hothouse I broke into. Speaking of which, the lead investigator of the infamous Hothouse Caper (the one who figured out I broke in, within five minutes of interviewing me) lived a couple blocks from Island Park. His son, Flipper, and I became good friends. I would be remiss not to mention our camping adventures in this story. I could easily write a book on those alone. On a side note, I recently learned Flipper passed away back in the 90s. God, I miss him. I am so sorry we never got to meet up as adults to reminisce about those days. Those sure are some great memories. I will always miss you Flip.

Anyway, this was back when Grizzly Adams was on TV. At the time, it was really the only show worth watching. Either one of us could have told you that. Flipper was two grades ahead of me and was already an avid outdoorsman when we started hanging out together. He had all the neat camping equipment too- a framed backpack, tent, sleeping bag, a buck knife, BB gun, you name it. He also had traps. In the interest of keeping this book palatable, I will skip the trapping stories. Let me just say I trapped, skinned, and stretched my share of critters. In those days we could sell the pelts to the local ACE hardware store. We'd use that money to buy more camping equipment. As usual, my life was an adventure.

Most of the time when we went camping though, it was just to be outdoors. When we felt ambitious enough to make the five-mile bicycle ride- or could talk Flip's dad into driving us, we would go out to the *boy-scout property* at the state park. But we also had a couple of smaller places to camp and trap within walking distance of our houses. As strange as it may sound, the best one was behind the city dump. It was adjacent to the Cavalry Cemetery and an easy walk, even with backpacks on. We were die-hard campers too. We even went *polar bearing-* that means camping in the snow. Most trips doing that were so cold we couldn't set up a tent if we wanted to. We just buried our sleeping bags in the snow.

One night I laid my bag out next to the warm, cozy fire and didn't notice the frozen puddle of water I was setting it on. Blanca, bless her heart, always slept at the bottom of my sleeping bag, curled around my feet, and panted. She was my personal space heater. That night, however, she climbed up and started nudging my face with her cold, wet nose. Annoyed, I tried to shove her back down to the bottom of my bag, but she wouldn't have it; that's when I felt her wet fur.

I climbed out of my bag cursing, put fresh wood on the fire, and woke up Flipper. Bless his heart; he was a real sport about my predicament. We spent the rest of the night taking one-hour shifts in his mummy's sleeping bag. While one guy slept, the other kept the fire burning. And whoever got the bag, also got Blanca- *The Heater*. That was the coldest night of my life. I still went polar bearing after that; I just paid closer attention to what I laid my sleeping bag on. Lesson learned.

I liked being out there so much, some days I would go there after school with Blanca and make a small fire out of sticks, just big enough to heat a can of chicken noodle soup. I would eat that while overlooking the Chippewa River with Blanca. Then we'd walk home.

Life would have been all right if I could have stayed out of trouble. My brothers did, for the most part. Sure they got in trouble from time to time (everyone does) but with me, it was like an irresistible compulsion; like shooting Ray with my BB gun- I just couldn't help myself. When confronted by a risk-to-reward scenario, my mind can usually see the best choice to make, but God loves me, I usually ended up doing whatever option had the most risk or sin involved. And by the end of eighth grade, I was back to doing that with conviction.

# Chapter 5 Get Rich Stupid

I had started out as a shoplifter... and not a very good one at that. But that was grade school stuff. I was in junior high now. It was time to upgrade my crimes. My friend Charles (a black man in his early twenties) and I had a B&E gig at a bar next to his house. The Avalon Bar is for those *townies* who remember. Many times, after it closed for the night, we would sneak in through the basement window. It had a piece of steel welded across it to keep intruders out. Well, it may have kept out normal-sized intruders, but Charles and I were both skinny enough to bend, contort, and squeeze our way past. Once inside, whoever got in would drop the brace from the back door and let in the other guy. Charles (he hated being called Chuck so I only called him that when I was mad at him) insisted we limited our steeling to beer and booze. We never touched the small amounts of cash. We stayed faithful to that rule and when we left, someone would stay behind to put the prop back behind the door. Then they would shimmy back out through the basement window. We would replace the insulation over the window and leave it exactly as we found it. This way no one would know anyone broke in. Yeah, we were always broke, but we usually had beer.

"I know how we can get some bread, Blizz," Charles said one day over stolen beers. He told me how he used to be a custodian at the Mt. Pleasant Public Works building. He claimed they always kept a generous petty cash fund in an unlocked drawer. With no alarms: we had but to crawl through a window, open a desk drawer, and leave-green as Christmas. Easy kabeasy! It always is, isn't it?

# It's All In The Shoes

The Public Works building was set between the city dump and Calvary Cemetery. Even though the front was an open parking lot, it was surrounded in the back by a six-foot chain link fence with barbs running along the top.

We came in through the cemetery and found a spot near the front where we could crawl under the illogical fence. Being clever bandits, we left a change of shoes so our footprints wouldn't match the crime scene. Of course, that was relying on an exit where we came back to the same place, changed shoes, crawled back under the fence, and left our crappy shoes behind. Things didn't work out that way, however, and I never did see my good shoes again.

We casually walked to the back of the building and by luck (or the will of God) found an unlocked window. It slid open and we crawled inside, with considerably more ease than the bar window where we used to steal beer. But during this gig, we tripped a silent alarm- that Chuck assured me they didn't have, and unaware of that, set out to find the cash. And as I recall, in no particular hurry.

I can't remember if the drawer was locked or empty, but we searched that office for a good ten or fifteen minutes before deciding the only thing worth stealing was a plastic, see-through coin box that was strapped to the side of a vending machine. It looked plenty *smashable*. We just needed to find a good smasher. Charles found a fire extinguisher that looked well suited for the task and was carrying it to me when red and blue lights lit up our abandoned parking lot.

We froze. The window we had come in faced the rear parking lot and the cops, so we ran towards the front of the building to escape. Unfortunately for Butch and Sundance, all the doors and windows

31

were key-locked. It was like a prison. How did we find the ONLY unlocked window when we broke in? We ran back and forth in that rectangular building, bumping into each other, ricocheting off each other, and screaming things that didn't make sense as we scrambled from locked windows to locked doors.

# Bad Timing

For some reason (I will never understand) I picked that particular moment in my life to have an out-of-body experience. I was watching Charles and I from the ceiling. We looked like cartoon characters, running around, bumping into each other, and bouncing off walls. We were like two pinballs. For some reason, that was absolutely hysterical... so I started laughing.

I don't mean I giggled or snorted; I mean I went into an all-out laughing fit. I knew the timing was bad (to say the least) but I couldn't stop. I know Charles wanted me to continue running around with him, screaming, but I just couldn't. I couldn't do anything but laugh and apologize for laughing.

After my fit subsided, holding my sides, I walked to the window to surrender. There was no use trying to escape this building. Charles had even resorted to throwing a chair against a window to smash our way out. All the chair did was bounce off the wire-lined security glass. And for some reason, that was funny too.

At that point, I decided to go out smiling and walked to the window with my hands up, ready for badges and guns. But the lights were gone. The parking lot was empty. "Come on Charles, they're gone!" I exclaimed. My laughing fit was over, and so was this party; it was time to leave.

We crawled back out the window and were amazed to see an empty parking lot. We looked to where we had left the shoes, but that was towards the front. We needed a speedy retreat out the back. Without speaking, Charles took off his shirt, wrapped it around his arm, and looked at the foreboding fence. I did the same, and we ran.

I don't remember climbing up it. I don't remember going over it, but seconds later we were both on the other side of that fence and running through the cemetery. We ran to the other end and climbed under the cemetery's illogical fence.

# Left or Right?

Once on the other side, we had two directions to choose from. This was the same area I had spent countless trips camping with Flipper and Blanca, so I knew it well. If we went to the right, we went back to Old M-20 and traffic. If we went to the left, we went to the Chippewa River and solitude. From there we could float down the slow-moving Chippewa until we came to Island Park. That would put us about two miles from the crime scene. We could get out near the bridge and walk home. Wet, but free.

Walking out to M-20 was risky, but that was the way Chuck wanted to go. "It's not even swimming, really. It's just floating," I tried to explain. "There is no chance they will look for us on the river. It's a guarantee we won't get busted if we take the Chip!"

I don't know if Chuck couldn't swim or if he just didn't want to get wet, but in the end, I went with his idea and we walked out to the road to hitch a ride. Wouldn't you know it, two blue and white cars immediately stopped to offer us one.

The officers told us a nearby building had been broken into and they just needed to see the bottoms of our shoes... you know, so they can rule us out as suspects. Charles had on his house slippers with smooth bottoms. They shined their flashlight on his tread-less soles and one of them said, "Yep, it's them."

Without further discussion I was handcuffed, read my rights, and placed in the back of a state police cruiser. They put Chuck in the other.

# Chapter 6 Homes Away

## Welcome To Foster Care

Two weeks later I was back in front of The Honorable Judge Personality. "Welcome back Mr. Blizzard. It's been a couple of years. It's my understanding that things aren't going so well at home, living with your mother?" he asked/stated.

I nodded.

"It's also my understanding that you don't want to live with your father?"

My dad was in the courtroom that day. He had never asked me to live with him. He didn't even notice when I was gone to Eagle Boy's for over a year. I didn't have the heart (or the nerve) to turn around and ask him if I could move back to Millbrook, so I simply said, "That's right."

"In that case, Mr. Blizzard, I am placing you in the Michigan foster care system. Good luck and blah, blah, blah." Gavel.

## Down On The Farm

The first place I was sent to live was the Sazma farm. It was a temporary foster home- designated a shelter by the state. They kept kids for up to thirty days until a permanent home could be found. My first time there lasted nearly the full month allowed. Then I was placed in a permanent foster home- that turned out to be not so permanent. It's also where I had my first Intermonial.

# (Intermonial #1)

As stated, an Intermonial is a divine physical intervention. When I saw God in that van at Eagle Boy's, it was just a feeling; it was an understanding of how being in Eagle Boy's was where God wanted me to be. I felt God had put me there. Or more exactly, like God had seen I was put there. He somehow had His hand in the minds of those or a hand in the things that happened, brought me to Eagle Boy's. Nothing actually happened. In an Intermonial, the event can be as ordinary as words spoken, but by definition, something needs to physically occur. That didn't happen at the Village, but it sure happened at my first foster home. Before I tell you what happened, I have to tell you about a thought I had about a week before this incident. I even remember where I was in that little town, smoking a cigarette, when I had this thought. It is clear in my memory and relevant as I look back on the event.

I was having that smoke I told you about down the street from the foster home I was staying in when I came to this conclusion about people who don't believe in God and why God would send them to hell for denying 'He is real.' God doesn't physically show Himself, so how can He justify eternal damnation if someone doesn't accept that He is real? I thought about my time in Eagle Boy's and now my time here and how everything seemed orchestrated by a Higher Power. I couldn't be the only one this stuff happened to, so if it happens to others and they ignore it, that means they really are denying the obvious. It is no wonder God sends them to Hell.

What happened next must have been within weeks, perhaps days, of that thought. It was as if God was answering my theory on Him by doing exactly that- showing Himself to me through events that happened in my life. Skeptics would dismiss this first Intermonial as mere coincidence. That is easy enough to do, but it wasn't. As always, you are invited to decide for yourself if the following was a divine intervention or not, but I knew it was God then just as I know it was God now.

# God Called

To tell this part of my story, I must walk a delicate line. WARNING: there is kind of a sex scene coming up. I say 'kind of' because there isn't any actual sex, but it sure comes close.

It was with my first foster parent's daughter, *Mayhap*. I was in ninth grade, she was tenth. She was beautiful. And for some reason, she liked me. At night when everyone was asleep, she would often sneak into my bedroom and crawl in bed with me to hug and kiss. She was a virgin and wouldn't let it go any further than smooching, but since she was the most beautiful girl I had ever kissed, the sexual torment was fine with me. Well, it was tolerable.

Then came the day her parents left us alone. It was Saturday and they went shopping in a neighboring town. I saw it as my chance to be Mayhap's first lover. We were finally alone, without her parents sleeping downstairs. Within a few minutes of them driving away (perhaps just one), I had her in my bed.

The petting turned heavier than ever and at one point she whispered in my ear, "Why not?" That was all the green light I needed. I pulled down our sweatpants and was an instant from consummating our relationship... when the phone rang.

"Stop!" She gasped, stiffening. "That could be my parents. Go answer the phone."

"So what?" I said, ignoring her plea and continuing my quest. "Let it ring."

"No! Stop! Go answer the phone!"

"Aye, aye, aye!" I cried and pulled up my sweatpants. Under extreme protest, I got out of bed, assured her I'd be right back, and then huffed downstairs to answer that blankety-blank phone. "Hello?!" I said, rougher than I should have- in case it was her parents calling.

"Hey Blizz! It's me, Bob."

I responded with silence.

"I bet you didn't think I'd be calling, huh?"

More silence.

"You there, Blizz?"

"Bob?" I asked, bewildered. He was a good friend in sixth grade and lived a half-mile away from me. Back then and I don't remember him ever calling my house. Not even once. Bob just wasn't a phone guy.

At the time he called, we lived at opposite ends of the county. I had given him my phone number about a month earlier when we ran into each other while I was visiting Mom. Now, of all possible times, Bob decided to call me. I don't remember what I said to him, but I know it wasn't nice. As I think back, I don't think we've spoken since that day. I know it was a quick conversation. I hung up and ran back upstairs-

hoping Mayhap would be ready to continue.

She wasn't. She was dressed and in her own bedroom. I tried to go in to talk to her, but she had clearly settled down. She was wearing jeans, and a sweater and brushing her hair. She ordered me out of her bedroom and closed the door.

# Bargaining With God

I went back to my room, fifteen years old, horny and upset. I wasn't angry at Mayhap for regaining control and sending me away. I wasn't angry with Bob for calling. I was angry with God. He made Bob call. I knew He did.

I went for a walk by the millpond behind our house to yell at God. And yell at Him, I did. I don't remember what I said, but I do remember blaming Him for ruining my moment. Towards the end of my fit, I even offered Him a deal by promising to not get her pregnant... if He would just let me have that moment back. "Come on God, please?" I begged.

It was no use. God had His plan. And it was NOT for me to continue a relationship with my Mayhap. I was not wearing protection. Had we gone through with our tryst; it could have easily turned out a lot worse than a relationship ending badly. Her parents, God bless 'em, were devoted Catholics. I have no idea what they would have done with a pregnant daughter and the foster kid- who was responsible for it- living with them. Shutter the thought. Undoubtedly, my life would have turned out a lot differently.

# She Moved On

To wrap up this part of my story, within a week of *God's calling* she was dating a senior. She told her parents about her and me. She also told them that she wanted to break it off with me; which she did, but that I didn't want to break it off with her, which I didn't. Suddenly I was an ex-boyfriend who lived in their house. That made me as unwelcome as... as an ex-boyfriend living in their house. They called my caseworker (Mike Mills, one of my guardian angels) and told him to come over that day and pick me up. It was time for the ex-boyfriend to leave, now, that day.

# Back On The Farm

Just like Eagle Boy's Village was full when I arrived, so was the foster care system when Mayhap's family sent me away without notice. I found myself back at the Sazma farm. It was by far, my best teenage experience. Actually, other than raising my kids, living on that farm, were the best days of my life. The best so far anyway.

It was a traditional family farm with about 130 acres of cropland. They had cows, chickens, and sheep. It had a big old-fashioned barn with haylofts and a rope to swing on. There was a swimming hole in the backyard where ducks swam and fish jumped. In my mind, it's still a postcard. In the mornings I would walk past the pond and pick a couple of ears of corn. The sheep would see me, bah, and run along the fence, following me. They would push and shove each other for their share of freshly shucked corn. After everyone got a mouthful directly from my hand, I would toss them the rest while saving a pocketful for the wild ducks that lived in the pond.

"QUACK! QUACK! QUACK!" The ducks had their *feed me-quack* like the sheep had their *feed me-bah*. I would sit down and two ducks (husband and wife I assume) would waddle up, gabbing away. Just like the sheep, they would eat out of my hand. But their nibbling duck beaks were a welcome change to slathering sheep tongues. The best part was, they were wild creatures. They weren't domesticated like the sheep. Just from watching me feed the sheep, they accepted my morning walks as part of their life. Occasionally, one would even let me pet it.

The Sazma's made a special request for the state to let me stay past the thirty-day limit so I could finish the ninth grade without changing schools again. Dear Don and the late Sue Sazma, I thank you with all my heart. You are two angels that God blessed me with during this crazy life. I love you both.

I stayed there for three months so I could finish ninth grade. At the end of the school year, Mike found me a foster home in another county. Moving a foster kid out of jurisdiction required special permission, but he got the paperwork pushed through so I could go live with *Jim* and *Lulu Crab* of Hemlock; about thirty miles away from Mt. Pleasant.

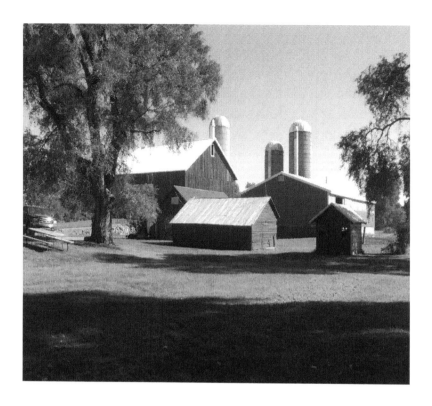

The Sazma farm as it looks today. Sue is passed, bless her heart and Don has moved away, but Dave still owns and runs the place. It IS still a postcard place to be.

# Chapter 7 Weekend At Work Camp

I went to stay with the Crab family as a trial visit my first weekend after finishing ninth grade. Making it a 'trial' visit, would make a 'no thank you' less awkward for either one of us if things didn't work out. Mike dropped me off on a Friday at their three-bedroom ranch home in the country- about five miles from the small town of Hemlock. When I arrived Jim and his son, *Buford*, were busy mixing and pouring cement to add a slab of concrete to their ever-expanding driveway. We said our hellos and I was handed a shovel and told how many scoops of dirt to mix with a shovel full of Ready-mix concrete. I told Mike I'd see him on Sunday and waved goodbye with the tip of my shovel.

After about three hours of digging, mixing, and spreading concrete, we cleaned tools and straightened the driveway. At one point I asked Buford, "Do you normally work this much?"

"Oh no," he assured me. "Tomorrow we are going up to the cabin. Then you'll see how much fun we usually have. Do you like to fish?"

Side note: I haven't shared any fishing stories with you, but let me assure you I could write at least one REALLY big book of them. I discovered carp fishing on the Chippewa River when we first moved to town and pardon the pun, but I've been hooked ever since. Buford told me that we could bass fish from their boat at the cabin the next day. Wow, I liked this guy already. We woke up the next morning to a big breakfast, loaded up the station wagon, and rode up north to the cabin with Jim and Lulu.

I drooled at the fishing potential as we drove down the dirt road that ran the circumference of *Links Lake*. At a branch in the road, however, we pulled into an older cabin that was on a smaller lake. Still, it was the nicest place I'd ever seen. It had two little bedrooms and an attic that acted as a third bedroom. To me, it was paradise.

Once we got unpacked, Buford pointed through the pine trees to where their boat was beached on Lake *Crapalot*. "I will take you down and show you that later," he said; "if we have time. Here's a shovel. We need to dig a basement. Make sure you wear gloves. You'll be sorry if you don't. Grab one of those wheelbarrows and follow me."

"You're kidding, right?" I asked, sincere as sunlight.

"I wish," he said, shaking his head. "I bet it seems weird to work so much, huh?" he understated and continued. "Usually we don't have projects going at both places at the same time. I'm sure we'll get in at least an hour of fishing before bed. Maybe we can even go again early in the morning before Dad wakes up and puts us back to work. Come on. This basement ain't gonna dig itself."

# The Eternal Basement

So we dug. We dug all day. We filled wheelbarrows with sand and hauled and dumped them in the back yard. Then we dug some more. The thing about digging in sand; is every time you remove a shovel of it, fresh sand (from somewhere?) immediately flows in to fill what you just removed- nullifying your progress. It is absolutely maddening to haul out a wheelbarrow of sand and return to see no progress. None! Just load and dump the wheelbarrow, then come back for another. Any mathematician will tell you that if you keep removing sand, it has to end at some point. Well, it never did. As a matter of fact, I don't think

that basement is done to this day.

We did get in some fishing that night, however... about thirty minutes on Lake Crapalot. Then it got dark and we had to be in bed. We needed our rest for Sunday. That basement wasn't going to dig itself. I swear; that basement wouldn't dig itself if you helped it.

Sunday came and I found out Buford was right about me being sorry for not using gloves. I took them off when my hands overheated the day before. Now I had two palms full of blisters to remind me not to do that again. The leather gloves went back on and I worked through the pain. We only dug for a few hours. Then we loaded up and drove back to Hemlock. The Crabs called Mike Mills and had him pick me up.

"How was the visit?" he asked me during the drive back to the Sazma's.

"I worked a lot," I said, looking at my hands. Mike noticed them too.

"I remember they stuck a shovel in your hands when I dropped you off on Friday. Did you go fishing at their cabin?"

"I went there. We drove around the lake, so I know I know it exists. But I sure didn't get much fishing in."

"Well, aside from all the work, did you have a good time?" I could feel his exasperation. I was whining. He spent a lot of extra effort to find me a family he felt was right for me. He even had me transferred over county lines. Now here I was, looking at a few blisters and complaining.

"I had a great time," I said, honestly. "The Crabs are good people. Score on them having a cabin, huh? They can't work all the time.

45

Sooner or later they have to enjoy all the things they have. I hope I'm there when they do. This is a great foster home."

 "Next weekend you're set to have another trial visit. Do you think we need another one?"

"Not unless they need another test run on me. I'm ready to move in with them any time," I said, knowing I had found a good home.

Mike called the Crabs on Monday. They thought we were a good fit also. The following week I said goodbye to the Sazmas, my farm, my sheep, and my ducks. On Friday, Mike dropped me back at the Crabs... this time to stay, for a few years anyway.

# Chapter 8 My New Life

## Cast of Characters

In a way, they seem like characters now, but they were, at the time I'm going back to, family. Jim and Lulu were like a new Mom and Dad. Not replacements, mind you, just additional parents; married parents that lived together and talked to each other. Their kids were like a new brother and sisters; again, not replacements, just *additionals*.

## Jim

Jim was really the nearest thing I had to a father figure. When my folks divorced I was too young to develop many memories with my real dad. With Jim, on the other hand, I spent a lot of time, during my high school years. He was smart and funny, like me. He usually dominated the conversation and was the focal point of the room. I will do my best to depict him fairly. He had/has his faults, like anyone; I just hope they don't overshadow his decency of the past. At one time he was very good to me. At one time.

He was the consummate businessman and worked Monday through Friday at the delivery business he bought from his dad. He had left for work most days before I woke up and would come home between five or six in the afternoon. The guy was a perfectionist. He demanded and often got, things just the way he wanted them. If things weren't that way, he would let you know. As a matter of fact, he would let the whole world know. I wore my heart on my sleeve, and Jim wore pain on his. Along with anything else that happened to be bothering him at the

47

moment.

His tongue was a poison-tipped spear that he was never afraid to use. Actually, that was usually the first thing he used when he disagreed with someone. He harpooned everyone, not just his wife, son or me. Well, everyone except his daughter, Clog. Of course, she never did anything wrong, so perhaps she deserved special consideration.

Buford and I sure didn't. For instance, once we spent the entire day working around the house cleaning the garage, tilling the garden, cleaning the dog pen, and mowing the grass- just to name a few things we did that day during summer break. When Jim walked in the door from work, Buford and I were watching TV on the living room sofa. I knew he would be stunned at how much work we accomplished. I even left the garage door open so he could see how organized and clean it was. I was prepared to humbly accept his accolades with, " Aw, shucks, glad to help out."

Instead of walking in the door full of praise, however, he walked in the front door and yelled all down the hallway, "Why the hell are there two GIANT weeds out by the telephone pole? Was it too much trouble to pick 'em or are you guys hoping they'll grow into trees? Gee, I hope I'm not interrupting your break. Comfy?"

It didn't take long for Buford and me to learn that when we saw him pull in the driveway; we headed to our bedroom.

# Lulu

Lulu was the Yin to Jim's Yang. She was the other half, the nice half. Buford and I went to her when we wanted something. As a rule, Jim said no and Lulu said yes. Jim was the stressed-out, grouchy businessman and Lulu was the sweet, loving housewife. She managed the house, cooked the meals, did the laundry... and said yes to us kids.

Best of all, she listened. It didn't matter how chaotic life was, when she sensed something was bothering you, she would put the world on hold to hear your troubles. While Jim cared what you did, Lulu cared how you felt. It was a good balance.

# Buford

My new little brother and I clicked almost immediately. I had six brothers so I was used to them. All he had was an older sister. Now he had a big brother; something he never had before. I had a little brother; something I had never had before. During the time I lived with the Crab family, he and I became like real brothers. We shared everything from movies to music. We liked the same everything. We talked about which girls did and which girls didn't. We shared all the things important to teenagers. We were brothers, once.

We even played the same sports together. We ran Track and Cross Country, which was his idea. He thought to be cool; we needed to be in sports. I played three seasons of baseball as a kid, but Buford liked the co-ed aspect of running sports. "Man, if we play baseball," he explained, "All we get to hang out with during practice is a bunch of dudes. In Track and Cross Country though, everyone works out at the same time; chicks and dudes."

I had to concur. So basically, we joined those sports so we could be around girls.

# Clog

Buford may have been like a brother, but Clog was never a sister. I certainly didn't see her as a sister the night I made a pass at her. Like Mayhap, she was a grade older than me. She was also a bit scrawny with a 'Miss Goody-two-shoes' attitude, but she was still kind of cute. Not long after moving in, I got drunk at a wedding reception and tried to kiss her.

At some point, I talked her into going outside alone with me. That's when- with a drunken grace I can only imagine lacked all suavity, I made my move. She said, "No way," ducked under my open arms, and ran back inside.

Thanks God! No, I wasn't looking for Him that night and I certainly wasn't happy about being rejected, but I did feel a huge relief that this foster home wasn't going to end because of a romance with their daughter. Of course, I have never been able to make her understand that. From that night and to this very day, she thought/thinks I was/am hot for her. Good grief.

Let me reiterate that I have changed the names of many people and places in this book. Some of those may be obvious, some not. Clog Crab, is one of those. I don't know if I need to point this out, but Crab is not her real name.

# A Good Life

After all of my bouncing around, I finally had a steady home with traditional parents. I believe what benefited me the most was having guidelines. From pulling decent grades in school to doing my chores around the house and at the cabin, there were rules I had to follow and things that were expected of me.

I had a good life. Heck, I had a great life. And after being the new kid at so many schools, I also knew how to make friends; usually by making them laugh. And God loves me, I've always had a knack for doing that.

Hemlock was a small town nestled in a farming community. Most of the people there were good, down-to-earth, country folk. But being twenty miles outside of Saginaw, it also had a more affluent, urban population mixed in as well. In short, Hemlock was a great town. It still is today. It maintains its small-town feel even though Urban sprawl has brought McDonald's and a traffic signal.

In school, I got along with all four of our major social clicks- the preppies, stoners, jocks, and geeks. I would have lunch with the preppies in the cafeteria, go have a cig with the stoners by the dumpster, then hang out with the jocks during Cross Country or Track practice after school. Even the geeks liked me because I made them laugh.

I smoked cigarettes and weed. Mostly just the stoners did that. But nearly all the kids in Hemlock drank. Me, I was a party-waiting-to-happen long before I came to live with the Crabs. But it was mostly marijuana. I didn't enjoy drinking as much as smoking weed. Even when Charles and I stole beer from the bar, he drank and I sipped.

The Crabs, on the other hand, were drinkers. To be fair, they were mainly weekend drinkers. I hardly ever saw them drink alcohol during the week. When I first moved in with them, Jim and Lulu would drink when we went up north to the cabin, but mostly it was just a few beers.

Jim would have them either while working on a project or B-B-Qing, but as memory serves, the first couple years I lived with them they didn't usually drink to excess.

By the time I was a senior in high school though, that was a different matter. More often than not, when they drank, they drank themselves drunk. They would come back from the bar fighting about one drunken subject or another. I even remember them fighting naked in the living room when Buford and I were sleeping up in the loft above them. I peeked over the edge to get a glimpse of the show, regretted that move, turned away, and went back to bed. Eventually, they got over Jim's brother hitting on Lulu, quieted down, and went to sleep.

I don't blame them for my drinking (that was always my choice), but it didn't take me long, living in that world, until I enjoyed drinking too. I reached the point that I drank almost every chance I could. Whether I was sailing, fishing, sitting at the beach, swimming, or watching the fire burn- pretty much any time after breakfast was acceptable up north drinking time.

# _High_ School

My senior year I was voted Class Partier 1985... and I have to say, I earned the title. Pretty much every time Jim and Lulu went away for the weekend, leaving us kids alone, I had a party. Most everyone, who was anyone, from school showed up; and we went wild with beer and pot.

I don't blame my drinking on the Crabs though. I honestly don't. I think they demonstrated responsibility by not drinking during the week. But since I was a high school kid, I saw drinking alcohol during the week not only as a right but also as my duty. Not drinking during the week didn't apply to high *schoolers*. That was a rule for adults.

But other than all the booze, I had a normal life; better than most. I had a new identity with a new family. Even running Track and Cross Country was very un-Chris *Blizzardish*. I loved my new school. I loved my new life. The Cracker Box on Maxwell Street and Eagle Boy's Village seemed a lifetime away. I even landed the lead role in our school play my senior year, A Hillbilly Weddin.'

# A Hillbilly Fiasco

Dr. Maxwell was my character. If memory serves, the basic gist of the story is that a doctor has car trouble while traveling through the boondocks and ends up marrying a country girl. I can't remember if it was a shotgun weddin' or if I fell in love. I just know I got drunk. Well, not as Ronald Maxwell, the doctor. I got drunk as Chris Blizzard, the guy who stepped outside during practice to chug beers between scenes. My good friend, Doc (who played a hillbilly), was right there with me, matching me beer for beer. One night we went through an entire case during a two-hour practice session.

After that practice, I drove home and went straight to bed. "Yeah, yeah, practice was fine'" I said to Lulu when I walked inside, completely blotto. "I'm really tired. I'm going to lie down for a minute." That minute turned into hours and I didn't get up until around midnight. I say I got up, but I didn't wake up. The next day Buford told me I woke him up because I was inside the closet banging around boxes and hangers; cursing like a sailor- a very drunken, confused sailor.

I don't know if it was Buford yelling or if I finally made enough noise to wake myself up, but I must have realized I wasn't in the bathroom.

I smashed my way free of the infernally small room and stumbled into the hallway. That is where I should have turned left, followed by an immediate right into the bathroom. Instead, I just went right and straight to Clog's bedroom window.

I pulled down my underwear and peed all over her brand-new pink and white curtains. I don't remember doing that, but I did see yellow stains running down them the next day. I do remember fidgeting with her window lock, like a toilet handle. The damn thing wouldn't flush. Frustrated, but relieved, I lumbered straight down the hallway and into Jim and Lulu's bedroom.

I remember lifting up the covers and seeing Jim's naked butt against the side rail of his bed. For some reason, I thought I was at Doc's house and he was the one in bed. Looking at his nakedness I thought, *Hmmm, Doc must sleep in the nude. He better hope I don't tell anyone at school about this. He would really be embarrassed!*

And with that bizarre thought running through my mind, I climbed into bed next to him. I put my back to his and started nudging him away from me with my elbows. There was enough room for both of us. He could *scootch*. No need to be a bed hog.

Jim woke up while I was elbowing his ribs and pushed/hurled me out of bed. I hit the floor unceremoniously. I got to my feet and looked at a very befuddled Jim and Lulu. And they were sitting up in bed, looking right back at me. Now I was awake.

"What the hell are you doing?" Jim demanded.

"Wrong turn," I said, honestly. And without further explanation, I went back to my bed and re-passed out.

# About Last Night...

The next day I felt panicky when Jim came home from work. I expected him to give me grief over last night's bed-invasion. I was all set to tell him I wasn't drinking at play practice and that I just got a little turned around heading for the bathroom. Instead of giving me grief, however, he took the incident in stride and said to me in a low voice, "The next time you wanna get in bed with me, wait until the old lady's not around, will ya?" Then he winked and elbowed me.

I was relieved he had turned it into a joke. I didn't want to lie to him about drinking. I didn't want any talks about that subject. I was still waiting for him to discover his whiskey bottles in the bar were mostly food coloring, the vodka straight water. Besides, I was in the senior play. I played sports. I did most of my homework... and all of my chores. I was pulling my weight. I was functioning just fine, *thank you very much*.

# Chapter 9 Cabin Fever

It was called either *going up north* or *to the cabin*, but both meant the same thing. During my first year with the Crab family, they sold the cabin with the bottomless basement on Lake Crapalot and bought a nicer one across the road on Links Lake. This one was built on a slab foundation (instead of wooden pilings) so it thankfully held absolutely no potential for a basement addition. It was on a point, amid a mix of other lakefront cabins that were mostly used by weekend visitors. That meant they were usually empty; giving my new little brother and me free rein of the Peninsula. So really, we had a backyard with thirty or so empty cabins. Among the sprawl, we played everything from the occasional game of Kick The Can to the more frequent BB gun fight. We were always careful not to shoot anyone's windows, though. And whoever had the 'pump' BB gun instead of the 'cock' gun, was only allowed to use ONE pump so it wouldn't hurt too much to get shot. OK, you weren't "supposed" to use more than one pump... but unless the guy was in sight of you, we each gave it at least one extra pump. *Guyhood* demanded it.

Buford and I invented a game we called 'stick golf.' We would hurl a stick (we each had our own three-foot tree branch with the bark shaved off and one end sharpened to a point) towards a randomly picked target; which might be the neighbor's wooden swing as the next 'hole' or a boat dock. The person who made his stick land (pointed end in the ground), within a sticks-length of the target in the fewest number of throws, won the hole. We played that game the most.

We each had our own dog too. Buford had *Wiggles* and I had Blanca. Wiggles was a squirrely Labrador retriever that was darn near as dumb as Little Red. At first, despite my pleas, Jim wouldn't let me bring

Blanca from my mom's house to live with us. For some reason, he was always against me and my love of dogs. In the end, however, Lulu convinced him that it would make their home feel more permanent to me if I had my dog. That was momma Lulu, always fighting for the kids.

Since cabins on our end of the road were normally vacant, we never chained or penned the dogs up north. They always stayed close to the cabin. I never had to worry about Blanca running away; she just wasn't the type. And since Wiggles never left her side, we didn't have to worry about her taking off either.

Between bird hunting, fishing, sailing, camping, water skiing, etc, I could write a book on the times Up North. I think it would be a good read too. When I go back there in my mind now, there always seems to be a BBQ going and folks laughing. "Have a beer!" someone offers. If no one does, I sneak one. An unguarded cooler is always fair game.

## Up North or The Cabin? Both Meant Drinking

Trips to the cabin certainly weren't all about getting drunk, but by my senior year, that was what everyone usually ended up doing. Jim and Lulu would often close the *Rifle Saloon* in town while we kids would hang out in someone's cabin or at the beach. If it was winter and no one had an empty place to party in, we went road drinking in someone's car. Either way, we found a way to get drunk. The measure of that night's partying success was judged by how bad we felt the next day... and how little we remembered.

Since most mornings I rose with the sun (no matter how late I drank or how drunk I got), weather permitting, I went fishing in our small boat.

I would stop at the beach and gather the empty beer cans and bottles from the night before. That would help me pay for the next night's drinking. In Michigan, they have a ten-cent deposit on empties so I could toss a bunch of *ten-centers* in my boat and usually get enough money to buy a case of *Buckhorrible* beer and another pack of smokes. Again, going up north wasn't always this way. It just seems like it was towards the end.

Let me say again, I blame no one but myself for my troubles or problems. Jim and Lulu gave me a good home. Yeah, they drank a little too much, but like I said, they kept it mostly to the weekends. They were wealthy and successful people. I was the foster kid who went overboard with my addictions. No one twisted my arm.

I will say though, they helped form my own wrongful understanding between drinking responsibly and being an alcoholic. I thought that, apparently, getting drunk wasn't just for the winos that slept in Island Park. Drinking is what successful people do too. If you were homeless and poor, then you had a drinking problem. Jim had a nice house, owned his own business, and made over $200,000/year; which in the 80s was considerable. He owned a cabin, and eventually his own airplane. He couldn't have a problem with alcohol, right? A simple gutter check would tell you that much. I couldn't have a drinking problem either, right? After all, I was still in high school.

When I graduated in June 1985, the Crabs held a graduation party for me. It was a great time. With kegs of beer, it was a fitting send-off for the class partier. Jim and Lulu also helped me get accepted to Northern Michigan University. Being in the foster care system and a ward of the state, I also had access to about every government grant imaginable to help pay for it. With wealthy foster parents helping me, I had the all-American college life waiting for me. I was truly blessed.

# River Rage

Then, in late June, came the four-day drinking binge that only lasted three days. It started on a Thursday, at the cabin, and was supposed to go until Sunday. But on Saturday everything changed. A bunch of us decided to go on a tubing trip down the Ausable River. We gathered up the inner tubes, and beer, and started a three-hour float. That day I started with a sunrise beer and by the time we were on the river, around noon, I was completely smashed.

I'm normally a happy-go-lucky drunk, but I wasn't that day. On this particular drunk, I got angry. This is where some fog rolls in. I honestly can't remember everything that set me off that day. Part of it was a girl I liked taking up with another guy, but most of it was just for some reason, I felt like an outsider. It was like I didn't belong. I'm not really sure what it was, but looking back now, what happened is in keeping with my propensity to tear things down, primarily myself.

For whatever reason (or combination of reasons) it may have been, I got it in my head that the only ones who really loved me were my biological kin. By the time we reached the end of our ride, I came to the drunken, pissed-off, decision that my life sucked.

I remember telling Doc to drive me back home. I was sick of this sh--! Whatever 'this sh-- was... and I wasn't going to take it anymore. I even slammed his car door hard enough to shatter the passenger window. On the two-hour drive from the cabin to Hemlock, I raved about something. Like I said, I don't remember what, but I went on a rant during that drive and told Doc I was moving out to Arizona to live with my 'real' brother, Matt.

"What about college? What kind of future do you see in Phoenix? Why?" etc. Instead of seeing his logic and calming down, I was fit to be tied by the time we reached the house. I was still cursing and carrying on when we pulled into the driveway. Then he said the words that sealed my fate,

"Blizzard, you're just being a drunken idiot. When you sober up, you'll see I'm right."

I don't remember my exact response (not that it would be suitable for print if I did), but I slammed his front door (hearing the glass rattle) stormed into the empty house, stormed to my bedroom, stormed to my bed... and passed out. The next day I woke up, sober. With my brain back to reality, I realized I HAD been a drunken idiot. Doc was right. Dammit!

## Unless I go to Phoenix...

I had put on a grand show the day before. To say I was being a drama queen is an understatement. I was being a violent/psychotic drama queen. I had thrown down the gauntlet. Now, to make up for my drunken rant, I had to pick it up, fix Doc's window, and admit he was right. Admit that I had been a drunken idiot. It would take a long time to live down that shame. *Unless you go to Arizona*, my mind countered. *You're eighteen years old. You're a man now. You are a man, aren't you?*

With that thought in mind, I packed a duffle bag and wrote Jim and Lulu a goodbye note. I don't remember what I said, but I'm certain it didn't make up for the last three years they had taken me into their lives, their family, and their home. Here I was putting a runaway note on the headboard of their bed and running off. Was that my *thank you* for them giving me so much? I went out to the dog run and said goodbye to Blanca. I held her face and kissed her... one last time. I put her back safely in the dog pen, got on my bike, and left. I didn't know I would never see her again. I had no idea.

# Chapter 10 Birdbrain

In this chapter, I'm going to tell you about another time I saw God. As always, you are invited to judge for yourself if it was Him or not, but what happens next, to this day, is about the *darndest* thing I ever saw. I will tell the story EXACTLY the way it happened and then give you my interpretation, but again I ask you to believe me. This book is true. Every word. What happens next is no exception. I don't know if it was God, Jesus Christ, the Holy Spirit, or my guardian angel, but what happened was divine. Of that I'm certain. By all means, decide for yourself what caused a bird to act the way it did, but this is what happened. Exactly.

# (Intermonial #2)

The roads around Hemlock are spaced a mile apart, forming a perfect grid for farming. I say that because after Birdbrain, I counted back how many of these I had crossed and figured I had gone less than five when he showed up. It would have taken me less than twenty minutes to turn around and go back home, put my bike in the garage, tear up that stupid goodbye note, unpack my knapsack, and spend the rest of the day lying on the couch, watching TV and nursing my hangover.

Yeah, I felt rough, but I looked good. I had on my favorite shirt. I was a smoker and it had two breast pockets to hold my cigs. It was greenish-blue and buttoned up the front, with a nice collar that made it look professional, but with a turquoise color that made it look casual at the same time. Yeah, my gut felt like a bag of crap, my head ached, and I was running away from people who loved me. Was I also running away from a promising future? Maybe, but I was entering adult life, dressed nicely. How bad of a decision could it be when I looked this good?

The road was deserted and there was only corn growing to hold my attention. That's probably why I noticed the birds land on a telephone wire three or four poles down the road. Staring up at him, I wondered how close he would let me get before taking off. At that time, I had spent about half of my life in the country and the other half in the city. There is a big difference between city birds and country birds. A city bird will let you walk right under it when it's perched on a wire or in a tree. A country bird won't let you get close. This was a country bird. Even though the wire was high and I was no danger to that bird, I figured he wouldn't let me get within a telephone pole's distance before flying away.

Surprisingly though, he let me get right in line with him before he lit off. Instead of flying away, however, that crazy bird flew straight at me! It was as if he was on a Kamikaze mission. The road was empty, so I instinctively swerved to the left to avoid the unsolicited attack. But he flew down to about six feet over my head and stayed with me. I swerved back to the right and he followed without missing a beat. Then I went back to the left. I don't remember how many times I zigzagged across the road trying to lose him, but it was at least three, of that I'm certain. And all three times he stayed right above my head, like an attack helicopter.

I decided this bird was more than annoying or weird; he was going to poop on me. So I started peddling as fast as my eighteen-year-old legs would go. I don't know how fast that is, but it felt like I was going about twenty-five miles per hour when I looked back, expecting to see that bird- lagging behind, but Birdbrain was still right over my head, pumping his wings and keeping up with me easily.

"Ugh!" I cursed, hitting both brakes as hard as I could. Between the tires locking up and the front brake tightening so hard that the back wheel came off the ground, you could say I stopped quickly. I regrouped and looked up again, this time expecting to see Birdbrain out in front of me, perhaps even looking back, but he was still right above me. Now he was backpedaling his wings and losing what little altitude he had. I would have jumped up to swat him if I hadn't been straddling a boy's bicycle. Before I could get off the thing and start swinging, however, he dropped a big white blob on the right shoulder of my beloved shirt and flew off.

Now I was on an empty road with my knapsack, ten-speed bike, several hundred dollars, and wearing my favorite shirt... with poop on it. I looked back down to where the chase had started and figured it lasted about a half-mile. That bird had the express mission of pooping on me (that was clear), but why the big show? I saw what a good aim he had.

The truth is, he could have hit me any time he wanted. He had the firepower.

## I was just trying to run away.

I got back on my bike and kept riding. A few miles later I stopped at a gas station, went in the bathroom, and washed off my shirt. By the time, I got to Mt. Pleasant, twenty miles later, my shirt was dry and the bird incident was fading into memory.

Mt. Pleasant is where Mom lived. I rode over to see her before I left for Arizona and got all the same questions from her that Doc had hit me with the day before: "What kind of future do you see for yourself in Phoenix? What's wrong with your life at the Crabs? What about college? Why? Why? Why?"

I don't remember what I told her. I've just always been headstrong. When I get something set in my mind, people who know me (for the most part) generally stand aside and let me do my thing. It's best that way. Mom and I hugged and said goodbye.

I rode my bike to the bus station, parked next to the building, bought a one-way ticket to Phoenix, and got on board. As the bus pulled out from the station, I looked at my abandoned ten-speed and wondered how long it would be there before someone took it.

I was really doing it. I was right yesterday. And this proves it. Doesn't it? Either way, there was no turning back now.

# Intermonial in hindsight...

Why the big show?

I hear God knows everything... If that's the case, and I'm quite certain He does; then God must have known I was going to get back on my bike and keep riding that day, right? So why did He bother sending that bird in the first place? Why waste His time or mine? Or the bird's for that matter.

After a long time to think about that question I have come up with four good reasons: In no particular order of importance, this is my take:

The first and most obvious is that God was telling me to turn around and go home. I'm not smart, obviously... after all, I was throwing away a promising future for no coherent reason. I was leaving on a bicycle from Hemlock, Michigan, heading for Phoenix, Arizona... come on, how smart could I be? Still, God took the time to send Birdbrain to tell me I should turn around and go home.

The second reason He sent Birdbrain was to tell me that even though I was going down the wrong road, He was going with me. I wasn't alone... even though I felt more alone that day than I had ever felt in my life.

The third reason... and this goes back to God knowing everything... is that He knew I was going to tell you about it one day. I'll bet He wants you to think about your own Birdbrain. He wants you to think about the times He showed Himself to you. Of course, He gave us all free will, but that doesn't mean He doesn't know what choices we'll make. He knew I'd write this book... and He knew you'd to read it. I believe that.

The <u>fourth reason</u> I believe He sent Birdbrain was because God knew I would see Him. If nothing else, He did it just for the pure joy of watching a mixed-up kid who was throwing away so much- the same kid who yelled at Him for the interrupting phone call a few years earlier, see Him again. I bet God got the biggest kick out of that.

# Chapter 11 Been Through The Desert

After coming off the fifty-six-hour bus ride to Phoenix, the first thing that struck me about Arizona was the heat. Dang! It was nearing the Fourth of July and Phoenix was an oven. By the time I got off the bus, a long-sleeved polyester shirt that went well with my dark jeans had replaced my poop shirt and shorts. Good grief. It's like I couldn't make a good decision if my life depended on it. And in keeping with that newfound attribute, I showed up, unannounced at Matt's door, nearly dead from walking in the heat. "I'm here bro!"

"What about the Crabs?" he asked. "What happened? Want a beer?"

"Lord, yes."

We caught up, over beers. I told him I still planned on going to college in the fall. For now, I would get a job to help pay the bills. "I still can't believe you just took off," Matt said a lot during our talk. I couldn't believe I did either.

During my first week in Phoenix, I called the Crabs to let them know I had arrived safely and was staying with Matt. A week later I got a goodbye letter from Jim. What I remember of his note was the ending. PS: You're on your own now. When life knocks you down, pick yourself up, dust yourself off, spit, and get back in the fight. Good Luck!

The letter hurt. But I bet the letter I left on their headboard hurt them a lot worse. I turned my back on good people, for no good reason. What did I expect, warm *fuzzies*?

# Work Hard and Party Harder

I didn't have a plan. I thought about being a movie star or a rock star, but I figured I would deal with that as it came along. Matt got me a job, as a delivery driver, at the print shop where he worked. We went through a host of roommates and apartments that year, but always stuck together- and kept the same jobs, and partied. Sure there was the occasional cocaine buzz or acid trip (and pot often enough) but there was always beer. There was always lots of drinking. Towards the end of my year in the desert, I needed at least a twelve-pack just to get to sleep most nights. Then I was up in the morning and off to work.

As Blizzards, hard work is in our DNA; it's simply encoded into our genetics. And Matt Blizzard is the hardest worker I know. Some nights we would drink until four or five in the morning. But no matter how much we drank or how late we partied, at seven o'clock Matt would be leaving for work. Some days I tell him to give apologies to the supervisor. I wasn't going anywhere. Matt, *The Machine*, however, was out the door. Now that I think about it, I don't remember Matt ever missing work- for any reason. Yeah, he could always dish it out and he could always take it. That is Matt Blizzard in a nutshell.

We were living the 'work hard and party harder' creed like only the young can. Party/work/party/party/party/party/work/party. That was my year in Phoenix, in a nutshell. Of course, bad things can happen when you're drinking. The worst was the death of Harry Winters.

## Playing The Dogs

*Harry* worked with Matt and I. He was in his mid-thirties and a *lifer* on running a press. He drank every day, smoked pot, and was always down for whatever drug was at hand. Basically, he was a great fit with the Blizzard brothers. He loved to play the dogs (greyhound racetrack betting) and talked Matt and me into joining him one night for an evening of drinking and gambling. The thing that made that night memorable was Harry grumbling nasty remarks to me or about me all night. Most of it seemed to occur at the end of the evening so I marked it down to drunk talk.

We did have a good time. Harry won by betting on Whacky Blacky (the dog's real name) in the last race. He bet it all on him to win and it did! "Always bet Whacky Blacky!" Harry howled. At least it took his mind off hating me; for a while anyway.

By the time we gave him a ride back to his apartment though, Harry was back to spitting out remarks about me. I honestly don't remember anything in particular he said, but the basic message was that I was a cocky kid that needed to be brought down a peg or two. To his credit, I probably was. I didn't think so. One of my knacks in life is my ability to get along with almost anyone. I just rubbed Harry the wrong way somehow. Maybe I reminded him of someone he didn't like. Maybe he just didn't like me. I don't know, but in the middle of a great time, he was seething over me for some reason.

# Drinks All Around

A few days after 'dog night', Matt, Harry, and I, took the company truck out to a neighborhood bar that was having some sort of drink special. My memory from the bar is hazy, but basically, it was a repeat of the dog night without the racetrack to interrupt our drinking. Harry's attitude towards me was worse this time, a lot worse than at the racetrack. And he was a lot drunker. My memory is going into fog now, but I remember drinking lots of beer and slamming lots of different colored shots. And Harry turns meaner with each one. He finally got so nasty that Matt and I called it a night and said we were leaving.

Of course, since we brought Harry, we also had to give him a ride home. After we left and on the way to his home, we stopped by a friend's apartment down the street from the bar and went inside to smoke a joint. I hoped it would calm Harry down. Instead of relaxing over a doobie though, he was fixed on teaching me a lesson... about something. He wasn't just saying things under his breath anymore though. Now he was yelling at me. I wish I could remember a quote to summarize what he was saying, but I don't. He just had it in for a young kid that he thought was too cocky. As promised I'm keeping this book true. If I knew what he had against me, I would tell you, but I don't. He was just bent on putting me in my place; whatever *place* that was.

I don't know if we even finished the joint, but we left. During our walk to the parking lot, Harry's badmouthing turned physical and he shoved me into the pickup truck.

"Stop right there!" Matt yelled. "F--- with my brother and you f--- with me!"

"I can handle this bro," I said. I didn't want this fight, but I wasn't ready to go running for protection either. Besides, I knew Matt had my back. Even if Harry got the better of me, Matt would stop him from messing me up too badly. Actually, Matt would beat the snot out of Harry. But Harry was my problem.

I don't remember exactly what happened next so I won't try to recreate something I don't recall... but Harry came at me. The next thing I knew, we were on the ground wrestling; like most street fights end up. I had Harry in a ferocious headlock and was pulling on his neck with everything I had. I used my legs to push my body into his chest. That not only kept him from throwing any fists, but it also kept him from breathing. My weight was keeping his lungs from expanding, while my right arm was cutting off his windpipe.

"Let him up, bro!" Matt yelled. "You won. It's over."

"Tell Harry," I said. "I'm not letting him go until he stops fighting."

"Rrret Rov Re! I'll rill roo!" Harry choked.

And so went the conversation with Matt telling me to let go, me refusing and Harry gurgling out one death threat or another. Finally, he quit fighting and promised it was over. I let him up but stayed on my guard- just in case it wasn't over. Sure enough, it wasn't over.

Harry was standing about five feet away from me, panting hard. He clenched his fist and informed me that 'it' actually had just started. No, whatever had been eating at him the last few days was not going to end with a submission hold in the parking lot. That wouldn't do at all.

Harry was a scrapper and would never have made such a rookie move sober, but he cocked his right arm back to throw an extremely telegraphed right cross... and charged me with both his hands lowered. I was drunk... and scared. I didn't want another wrestling match so I moved at him and threw my own right hook. The punch connected squarely with Harry's chin. Between the momentum of him coming at my punch and me going at him, Harry fell to his knees and went facedown to the ash fault.

Matt and I tried to wake him up, but it was no use. We figured with all the alcohol in his system, he was out for the night. We hoisted him into the bed of the truck and drove him home. Harry was still unconscious, but alive when we got to his apartment. Matt and I dragged him inside and put him on the couch. I propped his head up with a pillow so he wouldn't wake up with a stiff neck; we wished him well and went home.

## He Was Partying With The Blizzards

The next day Harry didn't show up for work. But at about ten o'clock the cops did. They said Harry's wife and son (a toddler about four years old) found him dead on the couch that morning. His wife told the cops Harry had been out partying with the Blizzards. Now the cops wanted to know what happened. Instead of taking us downtown for questioning though- as cops do in the movies, they asked Matt and me to drive ourselves downtown voluntarily.

Needless to say, our employer was not impressed. We told him about closing the bar, the fight, and driving Harry home in the back of the work truck. They didn't let me take the company truck home after that. Before that incident, that little delivery truck was my own personal vehicle. I drove it home every night, even though I lived across the street from work. I also had it every weekend; along with the company gas card. I must admit; that I never put one penny of my own money in the gas tank. That company perk died with Harry.

Bob, the owner, had managers drive us to the police station- in separate cars. Matt and I talked before we went downtown and agreed we would simply tell them the truth. That certainly made it easy to tell the same story. Well, two drunks recollection of the same story, but two honest drunks, nonetheless. We didn't ask for attorneys.

Harry's autopsy showed he had a broken neck, which caused his brain to hemorrhage. A week later the D.A. called to say he wasn't pressing charges against me. They saw it as clear self-defense and closed the matter.

It wasn't closed for me though. I was devastated. I couldn't shake the guilt. He had an infant daughter, a four-year-old boy, and a wife. He didn't deserve to die. He was just drunk. I'd been there many times myself. I didn't deserve to die either. If I did die, all I would be leaving behind is six brothers and two sisters; not a wife and two kids.

# Old Dogs New Tricks

I called the Crabs and told them about Harry. They were understanding and told me to let them know if I needed any legal help. They also hit me with the bad news; Blanca had run away. According to Jim, one day Buford let her out to clean the dog pen and she just wandered off and never came back. It was the *darndest* thing. He sure was sorry. As a side note- I don't believe a word he said. I suspected then and I am convinced today that the evil Jim Crab got rid of Blanca to punish me for running away. He is like that.

Since Mom had always taken care of her, I took it for granted that my foster family would also. You know, the family I abandoned. They didn't though. No, after all these years of staying close to home and never running away, one day Blanca just 'wandered off and never came back.' Old dogs are always learning new tricks though, right?

For years to come, I told myself she went looking for me. She saw me ride off that day in 1985 and that she went west, towards Mt. Pleasant, looking for me. That's where Mom lived. That was home. The poor old girl must have got lost trying to find me. That was the only explanation I could entertain, the only one I could stomach. The thought of Jim doing something to her was inconceivable, then.

# The Worst Laid Plans

Between Harry dying and losing Blanca, my life in Phoenix was not going as planned. Whatever *plan* that was. Luckily I had lots of drugs and alcohol to help me cope. Of course, I didn't see that drugs and alcohol were causing most of my troubles in the first place, but this wasn't exactly a reflective time in my life.

I had a 1971 Pontiac Lemans with a hopped-up 350 (the fastest car I've ever owned) and a good job (making $5.50/hour). My brother, Tony, had moved out to Phoenix in the spring of '86. That made three Blizzard brothers sharing a two-bedroom apartment. Side note: Never rent an apartment next to three Blizzard brothers. Well, unless you really like to party late... and often. In that case, they're the perfect neighbors.

The partying went on while Blanca and Harry swirled in my brain, Guilt and Remorse. They followed me everywhere. I took them with me everywhere. I guess I took them to work too (I might as well blame them) because I started screwing up.

I had begun working for *Snappy Dappy Printers* as a delivery driver when I first moved to Phoenix. When I wasn't delivering to the customers, I worked in the bindery department finishing printed jobs. Within two months of starting as a delivery driver and having no previous printing experience, I was running the bindery department and had a delivery driver who did my old job. Another side note: If you ever get a chance to hire a Blizzard, do it. They're good workers- every one of them.

I wasn't such a good worker in the spring of 1986 though. Sure, I worked hard enough, but my mind wasn't there. My mind was back in Hemlock visiting Blanca while on a visit from college...or leaving Harry at the bar, madder than ever, but alive. Or my mind was already home with a cold beer and twisting the first after-work doobie. Wherever my mind was, it wasn't at work.

I was cocky about my job because I was good at it. From operating the folder to cutting down stock for the pressman, I kept things running smoothly. To this day my favorite job was delivering printing to beautiful, grateful, secretaries. On a side note: God bless every one of them. Ok, so my mind might have been busy with that too, but I felt I was good enough at doing my job that I could let my brain ride on cruise control. That plan didn't work out too well, though, and I started making careless mistakes; like leaving a skid full of paper outside in the alley overnight because I forgot to bring it in after signing for it. Or going on deliveries across town and not taking everything with me... on the first trip.

I don't remember exactly what happened at the end, but I got into a manhood contest with the vice president. To make a long story short, he won. I quit and was unemployed with no unemployment insurance and dead broke. All I had was two good brothers.

Side note: Thank you Matt and Tony for supporting me during that time. I love you guys.

God bless their hearts; they both took care of me. They kept the rent paid, fed me, and even bought me smokes and beer while I looked for a job. I looked every day too. My very first job in town had been as a bagger at a grocery store... hem, excuse me... a courtesy clerk. I only did that for a week before Matt got me the printing gig. To me, finding a job was easy. That had been my experience.

Suddenly I found myself, a nineteen-year-old kid, competing for bindery jobs against people who had been folding, numbering, scoring, cutting, piercing, wrapping, and delivering printing longer than I had been alive. Needless to say, the printing angle didn't work. As it turned out, I had it made at my old job and just didn't know it. Isn't that the way it always goes? Do you see a pattern in my behavior? I'm sure, didn't.

Nearly two months of unemployment later, I was at my end. My brothers weren't at their end with me though. Bless their hearts. They both kept telling me to stop stressing out. "Just keep plugging away bro... you'll get a job any day. We got your back."

# Where Do I Sign?

I enlisted in the Army, truth be told because I couldn't find a job. I thought about applying for loans and grants and going to college, but I couldn't go to school during the day and then come back to Animal House to study at night. "The music's not too loud is it bro? How was school today? What are you doing studying? Have a beer! And crank the stereo on your way to the kitchen! What? I can't hear you. You need to talk louder!" Etc. In short, it was plain I wasn't going to school while I was living with Matt and Tony. It wasn't their fault... by no means. You know I don't blame anyone in this world for my troubles but me. From running away from home a year earlier to quitting my job without an unemployment safety net, all my problems were my own creation.

When I was out job searching one day, I walked into an Army recruiting center. The sergeant told me that the Army had just started a two-year enlistment program. "So I can enlist for two years, and if I want out after that, I can leave? No hard feelings?"

"With an honorable discharge and $17,000 for college," he said.

"Where do I sign?"

I did my official swearing-in at the Reserve base in Phoenix that July, with an official report date of 18 August 1986 in Detroit. I went back

78

to the apartment and told my brothers. And the party started.

# Saying Goodbye to Arizona

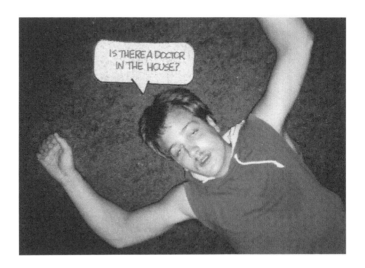

For some reason (that I will never understand) the main landlord of the five-building complex we lived in, took an apartment directly above the Blizzard brothers. How stupid is that?

During one of my goodbye parties that week, a bunch of us sat around the swimming pool with fishing poles and bobbers. We were blasting Pat Benetar when two female cops showed up.

Tony greeted them with a friendly hello and I asked them to dance. Blushing, ever so slightly (OK, maybe they didn't actually blush... that sounds like the fog talking) they asked us to calm down and explain why five people were fishing in the swimming pool.

"Because we're too drunk to drive to the lake," Tony explained. "Do you want us to drive to the lake drunk? Is that what you're telling us to do?"

"Sir, I'm telling you that you need to quiet down. The landlord called because of the noise."

We both turned to the apartment directly above us. The manager was out on the walkway in front of his apartment, shaking his fist. "Do you see what I have to deal with?" he asked the cops. "It's like this all the time!"

"Then why don't you move?" I asked. "You're sick of us having fun and we're sick of you bitching about it!"

"Sir—" one of the sexy cops began.

"Ma'am," Tony interrupted. "My brother is not a Sir. He is a Private. He just joined the Army and this is his goodbye party. He is going to serve his country. Not stand around bitching about people having a good time." He let his voice rise so our unfortunate landlord could hear. Then he turned back to our only female guests, "Wanna beer?"

"Wanna dance?" I asked again, opening my arms.

This time they did blush... and respectfully declined both offers. "Just keep the noise down, please. And thank you for your service, sir. I mean, Private. Good luck!"

After the pool gate closed behind them, Mr. Unfortunate started yelling at his wife. "The cops are leaving. That's just great! They're still down there fishing in the swimming pool, drinking beer, and smoking marijuana! I can smell it! But the cops think everything is hunky dory."

"Calm down honey, I hear one of them is leaving," his wife said to soothe him. But I didn't want him soothed. I wanted his head to explode.

"Who ya gonna call now?" I bellowed up to him and his unhappy wife. "Why don't you call your mom? Call your mom and ask her to come down here and save your miserable as--" He slammed his door and cut me off.

That was too bad. I just started my routine. If he had stayed out there a few more minutes, I'm sure I could have made him mad enough for his head to pop.

## Saying Goodbye in Michigan

A week and a harrowing drive across the country later in my Pontiac, I was back in Michigan with the Crab family. I had left a year earlier on my ten-speed. Now I was coming back in a '71 Lemans with no AC, a slipping transmission, four bald tires, a leaky such and such, and five worn-out thingamajigs. And the Crabs, bless their hearts, welcomed me back. No hard feelings. Amazing.

Blanca was gone. Everything else seemed the same. Even the bedroom I shared with their son was pretty much how I left it. I spent the next two weeks reconnecting with old high school chums... and staying drunk.

With the spontaneous departure, I had missed saying goodbye in style the last time I left, but I was making up for it now. The Crabs even went on a trip somewhere and left me alone with the house. God bless 'em. I said goodbye to Hemlock in true 'class partier 1985' style.

Somehow I survived on seven hours of sleep during my last three days in town. I even went on a canoe trip with Doc. The weather was warm and sunny. The water was perfect. The banks of the river were lush and green. The three-leafed plants along the riverbank were so soft I walked through them barefoot. It was a good time.

On 18 August 1986, the Crabs took me out for a farewell lunch and dropped me at the bus station. We said goodbye, properly this time. I was asleep on my feet and still a little drunk, but I was going away to the Army with a hug. Not leaving a note on their bed and riding off on my bicycle. Blanca was gone. I was drunk. Some things changed. Some things didn't. I found a lone seat in the back of the bus and passed out.

# Chapter 12 Back to Basics

In the last few days of my Hemlock goodbye, when I went canoeing with Doc and stopped to pee along the banks amongst those deep leafy plants I told you about... well, I probably wouldn't have mentioned it, and forgotten all about it long ago, if it wasn't for the poison ivy. I was at the 'in-processing' station where they issue uniforms and shave your head. From there, they assign you to a Basic Training unit. It was my first experience with wool socks and leather boots so initially I blamed it on that when my feet itched and turned red. It finally got so bad I asked to see a doctor.

"Oh dear," the nurse said when I took off one of my boots. By now my toes had been soaking in sweat for three days. The meat between them had died, turned whitish grey, and was falling off in globs. She put on gloves and grabbed a pair of scissors.

She snipped away the dead meat and handed me a packet of seltzer tablets and a plastic tub. "I want you to drop one of these tablets in the water and soak your feet twice a day in this bucket. That will help cure your infection. In the meantime, I need you to come back here every day so we can trim off more dead skin as it develops. Thank you. See you tomorrow."

I put my socks and boots back on, grabbed my plastic bucket and seltzer tablets, and returned to In-processing. I soaked my feet a couple of times and only made it back for my daily meat trimming once before I got sent to my basic training unit. Lord, what a day that was.

# <u>Not My Day</u>

I only have my own experience to draw on, but I suspect most soldiers have much the same first day of basic training. Well, the same start to that day, but I'll bet theirs ended a lot differently than mine though. With me, it usually ends up being a story. God loves me, my whole life's been that way. The first day of Basic Training was no exception.

They lined up about sixty of us outside one of the barracks, issued us 70 pounds of gear... and introduced us to four very angry drill sergeants.

Apparently, they had a right to be angry. Of all the new recruits they had ever seen, we were the worst. The Army had never asked them to make soldiers out of a sorrier bunch of ragbags than us. No wonder they were so upset. It just wasn't their day.

It sure wasn't my day. As a matter of fact, I will go ahead and speak for every recruit there and say it wasn't their best day either. Every one of us had an Army duffle bag (you know, the ones you can fit a Volkswagen into) strapped to our shoulders. And these were true duffle bags. Oh sure, they had straps to put your arms through so you could wear it like a backpack, but it didn't spread the weight evenly like a backpack would. Every one of those 80 pounds pulled directly on your shoulders.

Did you notice the pack already gained ten pounds? Well, it gained a lot more before that afternoon was over. It was August in Dixie; hot, humid, and sunny. We marched and got yelled at. We got to our barrack parking lot and got yelled at some more. We stood in formation drooling at our air-conditioned barracks and got yelled at some more. We baked in the sun for about two hours with those anchors breaking our backs. The drill sergeants had to have known how uncomfortable we were. They didn't care. They were too upset.

My feet itched. It wasn't as bad when we were marching. But now that we were standing at attention, I could wiggle my toes. They were downright uncomfortable. I thought about my little blue tub and seltzer tabs. I figured with my luck I wouldn't get a chance to soak my feet until after lights out. Too bad because they needed out of those suffocating wool socks and leather boots. I hadn't noticed the seltzer tabs doing any good, but just having my feet in cool water and air-drying them, did make them feel better.

Of course, that was back at In-processing. I probably wouldn't get much foot-soaking/air-drying time in now that basic had started. I just hoped my feet had soaked up enough seltzer water for the medicine to kick in and start working. It sure was squishy down there.

Finally, our drill sergeants calmed down enough to let us inside- but they never stopped yelling. They had us stand in front of footlockers and told us to stow our gear and be back outside in formation in fifteen minutes. "Exactly fifteen minutes!"

"YES, DRILL SERGEANT!"

# I got Time

My brain started doing math. I stored my gear for two minutes, grabbed my blue bucket and seltzer tabs, and headed for the bathroom. Giving myself time to fill the bucket, take my boots off, and soak. I figured I could get in seven or eight minutes without being late to formation. Something told me that this was not a good day to be late. I double-timed down the hallway, filled my bucket deep enough to cover my feet tossed in TWO seltzers, got in a stall, closed the door, and sat down to soak.

I was there for a blissful two minutes before a shiny pair of boots walked into the bathroom. I was hoping he didn't notice my feet soaking in a blue bucket, but he did.

He walked over to my stall door slowly, not knowing who was soaking their feet. I'm sure in his mind he was thinking that I must have been an officer. *Surely a Private- on day one of Basic Training- wasn't in there soaking his feet. The formation is in ten minutes. It must be a lost general.*

"Excuse me," he said in a hushed tone. He sounded nothing like the angry madman I had just spent the last three hours listening to. He actually sounded... well, normal. "Who's in there?"

"It's private Blizzard, drill sergeant," I replied in the same hushed tone.

"PRIVATE!" he exploded, back to yelling. "WHAT THE HELL ARE YOU DOING?" The shiny boots began pacing around the bathroom.

"SOAKING MY FEET, DRILL SERGEANT!" I was back to yelling too.

"WHAT THE---?" I'm not editing the sentence. He really couldn't finish his thought. "PRIVATE! QUIT SOAKING YOUR FEET AND GET IN MY OFFICE!"

"YES DRILL SERGEANT!"

That wasn't near enough soaking time. I dumped my bucket in the commode and went to put my boots back on- without air or towel drying my feet. I figured it would take me between ninety seconds to two minutes to put my boots back on. I looked at a wide-eyed private who had been in the bathroom through the whole exchange and asked him if I should take the time to reboot or just go straight into his office barefooted.

At first, the guy was speechless. He seemed as perplexed as Drill Sergeant Friendly. "I would put them back on," he finally advised. I looked at my green wool socks, heavy with grey meat pieces. My first temptation was to shake them out quickly before putting them back on. I picked them up to do just that when the meat started falling out of them on its own, forming a little pile of grey gook.

I'm sorry if that sounds gross. In reality, it's a whole lot worse than it sounds. If you have ever seen a dead dog washed up on shore after about a week at sea, then you have a vague idea of how the skin between my toes looked. Now take that same dead animal, wrap him in a damp wool sock, and seal it in an airtight leather bag out in the sun. If you have that vision, then you know what my toes looked like. Sorry again, but you have to understand how bad it looked to appreciate what happened next.

## Giggle Check

I scooped up the two little piles of dead meat and put them all in my left sock (My left foot was my worst), put my boots back on, and double-timed to the office.

I was scared and breathing hard when I walked up to the doorway. The door was open and three drill sergeants were standing behind a fourth who was sitting at his desk, grinning. They had been angry and yelling all day. Now they looked like school kids who had just shared the greatest, dirtiest, joke ever.

Obviously, they had all been talking about the private who was soaking his feet in the middle of Day One. That was a story they would tell their grandkids. "Private," the head drill sergeant began. "What were you doing in there?" At least he wasn't yelling. Actually, he couldn't stop smiling.

"SOAKING MY FEET DRILL SERGEANT!"

A sudden yip jumped out of all four of them and they elbowed each other.

"Why are you soaking your feet, private? Have you had a bad day?"

"DOCTOR'S ORDERS, DRILL SERGEANT!"

"Why did a doctor tell you to soak your feet, private?"

"I GOT POISON IVY, DRILL SERGEANT!"

"Poison ivy, huh? That's rough. It must be pretty bad (more giggles from the group). Why don't you show us what is so bad you have to interrupt training to soak your feet?"

I had been waiting for this moment since I first saw their grins. They couldn't stop smiling and jibing each other while I gave my lame answers. "DO YOU WANT ME TO TAKE OFF BOTH BOOTS DRILL SEARGENT OR JUST ONE?" I asked.

"Why don't you just start with one, private?"

"YES, DRILL SERGEANT!" I dropped to one knee and unlaced my left boot. From the corner of my eye, I could see them continuing to nudge each other, waiting for me to show them a red, itchy foot. Then the lead drill could explain to me that being uncomfortable was all part of being a soldier... blah, blah, blah. I bet they couldn't wait to tell other drill sergeants this story. Being that this was the first day of basic training, they certainly had their mean faces on, but I heard giggling... right up until I took off my sock.

I pulled it off slowly too, allowing my two-sock collection of dead meat to fall out in a pile. I stood back at attention and extended my foot. Then, for effect, I spread my toes.

They stopped giggling. They weren't snickering anymore. And I'm quite sure any plans for giving me the old 'soldiers need to endure pain' speech went right out the window. They were silent. Finally, in a weak far-off voice, the head drill asked me, "Does it hurt, private?"

It did hurt, but nothing like it looked. It was a steady throb, but tolerable. It looked like I had been the victim of some diabolical torture routine where acid was poured between my toes until I broke down and talked. And apparently, it had taken a lot to break me. Without the slightest grimace of pain, I said, "YES, DRILL SERGRANT!"

"You can't train like this!" he yelled at me. "He can't train like this!" he yelled at the other drill sergeants. "Take this man (I was a man?) back to in-processing until his foot gets healed. Put your boot back on private."

"Yes, drill sergeant," I said. I wanted to keep shouting, but that would have been like yelling at a funeral. I knew they couldn't take their eyes off me. I was savoring every moment. Before putting my sock back on, I began gathering the meat and looked for a trash can.

"Don't worry about that. I'll get someone to clean it up, private. Just put your boot back on and gather your gear. You're going back to the in-processing station."

"Will I be able to rejoin this unit, drill sergeant?" I asked, doing my best to sound like I really liked it there. I knew I couldn't come back to this unit, but I wanted him to hear how disappointed I was.

"I'm afraid not, soldier," he said with a sigh.

Now I was a soldier? I was a man? I looked at their faces, and God help me, I almost laughed. It bubbled up inside of me, but I somehow kept my poker face. I didn't show pain. I didn't show anything. My foot looked like I must have been in the most excruciating pain imaginable, but you sure wouldn't know it by my face. I was a rock.

I put my sock back on, laced my boot, and stood at attention, holding my soak bucket in front of me. I could feel them studying my face for any sign of pain. I gave them none. I know to this day those four drill sergeants have told that story countless times. And I know every one of them said petty much the same thing: *He must have been in incredible pain, but you wouldn't know it looking at him. He never complained. He just followed orders. Incredible soldier. The Army should have more men like him.*

"PERMISSION TO BE DISMISSED TO GET MY GEAR. DRILL SERGEANT!"

"Permission granted," he said, proudly.

I did the best about-face I could and left, making sure not to favor either foot. I went back to my footlocker, grabbed my 500-pound duffle bag, and walked outside.

# Thanks, Dad

Drill Sergeant Friendly was already waiting with a jeep to take me back to In-processing. I loaded my gear in the back and sat in the front. I don't remember what we talked about during the short drive back to In-processing, but he couldn't shut up. He turned into an honest-to-goodness Drill Sergeant Friendly. What I do remember clearly was the scene when he dropped me off. I got out and went to grab my duffle bag, but it was wedged between the backseat and the front. In my brief struggle to free it, he said, "Let me he—."

God bless him, DS Friendly started reaching for his door handle... and caught himself. He- a drill sergeant, was about to help a private with his gear. I bet he wanted to tote it up to the office for me too, but he stopped himself.

"I got it, drill sergeant," I said, jostling it free. "Thanks for the ride, Drill Sergeant."

Then he lost all professionalism. "Good luck, son."

Son? Did he just call me son? *Thanks, Dad*, wanted to jump out of me more than the laugh back in their office. But again, I was the stone. "Thank you, Drill Sergeant," I said. I could feel his eyes on me as I tossed the 1200-pound duffle bag over my shoulder and walked inside, making sure not to gimp. In-processing sent me back to the infirmary. This time I got Doctor Fixit instead of Nurse Snip-It.

"And you say she was trimming the meat and telling you to soak your feet in water?" He asked me, baffled. "Don't soak your feet. Put this cream on and keep your feet dry."

I spent the next week in bed, reading and air-drying my feet. I was glad to be back at In-processing. It was a series of wooden, WWII barracks scattered among pine trees. They were two-story and housed five bunk beds on either side of each floor- holding forty soldiers in all when full. Each house was a little different than the next. They had character. The 'foot-soaking' barracks was a brick institution. This was better. This fits me. This was actually the same one where they filmed a famous military movie. And that's a fact, JACK!

A week or so later my feet were healed and I was reassigned to a new unit that was just beginning the eight-week training cycle. It was down the street from In-processing in the same old-school-style barracks. Time to give Day One another try.

I don't remember that day, but I know I made it through without soaking my feet. And did a lot of push-ups. I did a lot of those for the next five weeks. Well, I did a lot of those for the next eight weeks, but on week five, they gave us a night off from training. That brought me a much-needed break... and Fatneck.

# Party Night

The rules for our night off were this: If someone came to pick you up (any civilian) you could leave base for the night. If no one came for you, you could have pizza, watch movies, and stay on base- with all the other losers. I wanted a night of smoking and drinking. I knew that wasn't on the schedule for anyone stuck on base. So basically, I needed someone to show up and claim me.

I was in Fort Knox, KY and everyone I knew was either in Michigan or Arizona. If I wanted someone to come bust me out for the night, I would have to bring someone from one of those two places. I had been enlisted for over a month and my first Army pay was in the bank. It would cost me nearly every cent I had to fly someone there, but it's not like I had anything else to spend it on. So to pay everything I had for a night of drinking and smoking seemed like a fair exchange to me.

Now I just had to figure out who I was going to call. I decided to try Fatneck. I knew her from high school in Hemlock and she was always nice to me. Maybe I should have seen her name as a bad omen, but just like that bird, I just kept right on peddling. Besides, she said the one word that sealed our fate. She said, "Yes."

God bless her, she was always good for a yes. She flew down to Kentucky to oust me for the night. And she was beautiful. Of all the days (and nights) we would spend together after that, I have to say she never looked better than she did on the day she walked up to our barracks.

# Fatneck and Frankenstein

To set the scene, Basic Training was a completely sealed environment. We never saw civilians. We never saw traffic. We never saw girls. We saw our drill sergeants and each other. That was it.

Our Week-Five day off was different. It was an open house with *Uncle Henry* and *Aunt June* stopping by to see *Little Joey's* living quarters. And with all my showboating and hot-dogging, everyone knew I had a girl coming. She flew out of Detroit with a bunkmate's wife and they both walked up to our barracks together. I and about twenty other horny GIs glued our faces to the windows when Fatneck and a very unattractive woman walked into view.

93

Fatneck was the most beautiful woman on earth that day. She wore a white blouse with a pink windbreaker. Her brunette hair was short and styled like she showed up for a photo shoot. She would have looked dynamite on her own, but standing next to my friend's ugly wife, she looked even better.

"Which one's yours *Blizz*?" a buddy asked

"The pretty one," I said.

Everyone cheered! Well, except Frankenstein's husband. He didn't cheer.

An hour later we were in a motel with a case of beer and waiting for the pizza man. What we did that night is blurry. I remember buddies from basic stopping by our room, lots of drinking... and more drinking. And how easy I was that night.

Blame it on the drink. Blame it on being locked up with nothing but dudes for the last two months. Blame it on being a young GI. Who cares? The night was great. We had a blast and everything went as I hoped.

The next day we hugged and said goodbye. I told her I loved her as she and Frank got on the bus to the airport. Three weeks later I graduated basic and was shipped to A.I.T (Advanced Individual Training) at Ft. Jackson, SC. There I could drink and smoke. And I did. I also learned how to be a Unit Supply Clerk (76 Yankee) while I was at it. Well, let me say I graduated anyway. I didn't learn much in AIT. In the middle of not learning anything, they graduated us two weeks early so we could go home for Christmas, and then straight to our permanent duty stations.

And where was my permanent duty station? It could have been

anywhere. I was a supply clerk. Every unit needs a supply guy. I remember a form I filled out at the recruiter's office. I was given my top five choices of states I would prefer as my permanent duty. I still remember my first pick. Hawaii. To this day, I still haven't been there. I don't remember what I listed on the other four, but I'm certain I didn't ask to be sent to the 187th infantry unit at the 101st Airborne Division, Ft. Campbell, KY. But somehow the guy (whoever *the guy* is) who hands out duty assignments must have discerned that is what I meant.

Over the holidays I stayed with the Crab family... and got together with Fatneck again. That was Christmas 1986 in a nutshell. What I remember anyway.

# Chapter 13 Military 101

I got to the 101 Airborne/Air Assault Division, Ft. Campbell, KY In-processing station in mid-January 1987. It was pretty much like the one at Ft. Knox with wooden, comfy barracks. I walked past the 187th Infantry one snowy afternoon- just to see what my new digs looked like. HHC Third Brigade Headquarters was brick and institutional, just like the foot-soaking barracks back at Ft. Knox.

I was given a sheet of paper with a list of about a dozen stations I needed to 'clear' before reporting to my unit. I was given ten days to get this done. Then I needed to report to my unit or I would be considered AWOL. Gee, wouldn't you know it took me every one of those ten days to complete it too?

It was cold and snowy when the bus dropped me off at HHC 3rd Brigade Headquarters, 187th Infantry. I think I even waited until around noon to get there. I figured with the day half over; they would assign me my room, tell me to unpack, point me at the chow hall, and tell me where and when to report in the morning. Well, that's the way it happened in my imagination. Here's what happened in reality:

## Did I Come At A Bad Time?

The wind nearly ripped the front door out of my freezing hands as I walked inside, set down my bags, and looked at the CQ desk. Normally there is always someone present to greet whoever comes in. On this day, however, the desk was empty. A moment later a group of soldiers worked their way past me, hauling something big, green, and heavy. "Who do I-" I started to ask. Before I could finish, someone grabbed my shoulder and spun me around.

"You Blizzard?" he asked/demanded.

"Um, yes sir," I said, staring at a silver lieutenant bar amid the commotion. The doors on the opposite side of the building were propped open to a courtyard jammed full of military vehicles. There were soldiers hauling and loading equipment of one kind or another; while the snow fell and the wind howled. Damn, it was cold.

"Where the hell have you been? You were supposed to be here over a week ago!"

"I had to go through a lot of stages and get a lot of sig-"

"Save it Private," he cut me off. "I know you waited until the last day to get here. You had your break. Break time is over. We're going on a three-week bivouac. Stow your civvies in that bedroom; grab your TA 50 (field gear) and get on one of those trucks. Welcome to 3$^{rd}$ Brigade."

# <u>Bad Dogface</u>

Since I didn't show up until my final report date, I was in the doghouse with those above me... which was everyone. And since I was at the brigade headquarters level, I worked directly around the top brass. Lucky me. The first day I helped erect tents and install heaters. The officers were given GP (General Purpose) Small tents that housed eight cots encircling a small kerosene heater. The enlisted had a rectangular GP Medium, which held twenty or so cots. That tent needed a much bigger heater, which they brought. After I helped get it burning nice and warm, right before dark, I was given two tarps and told to go set up a 'hooch' (a pup tent, or GP Tiny as it was jokingly called) for myself.

Thankfully they only made me stay out there (sorely missing my Blanca foot heater) two nights before letting me move into the enlisted tent. I think the only reason they even let me in the nice tent is because, after the latrine incident the following day, they figured I was so stupid it really might have taken me all ten days to in-process.

# Call of Latrine Duty

On our second day of encampment, Specialist Mauger and I were instructed to erect a screen latrine. We dug postholes and set up a half dozen posts. Once that was accomplished, we stretched the privacy canvas to create a mini field bathroom- a Screen Latrine.

After the tarps were stretched, the only thing left to do was dig a poop hole. That task was entrusted, naturally, to the guy who didn't report to his unit until the last day possible. Mauger, smiling, handed me a shovel and said, "Any questions on how to dig an official military poop hole?"

"Duh," I said and laughed. I remembered the dimensions from Basic Training. I wasn't stupid. Two rifles long by one rile wide by two rifles deep.

So I dug... and I dug... and I dug. If you've ever had to dig in Kentucky red clay (perhaps you lost a bet), you know I earned every shovel of earth I took out from that infernal ground. I was rightfully proud when I was done... even though I only went one rifle deep because of rocks and pine tree roots; it was still a big hole. It may not have been exactly up to spec, but you could have buried a man proper in it.

I finished and went to chow. On my way back to use the new latrine after dinner, I saw the full-bird colonel coming out of the latrine and raced up so we would cross paths. Maybe he would ask me, who dug that impressive hole? I didn't know if he was aware I had come to the unit at the last minute or not, but I figured any chance I had at having my hard work recognized by a colonel would be good for me. I couldn't help but smile when I saluted him, "Air Assault, Sir."

He didn't return my salute. "Private, who dug that hole?"

"I did sir," I said. Instead of pride, I suddenly felt like I was confessing to a crime.

"Holy shit, Private! How do you expect anyone to use that death pit? I about killed myself!" That said; he stormed off down the trail adjusting his uniform, mumbling and cursing as he went. It went nothing like the conversation I expected.

First Sergeant Freeman had been walking up when the conversation started but wisely ducked behind a tree until it was over. Once the colonel was gone, he popped out and asked in a low tone, "Blizzard, what was that all about?"

"I don't know, Top. I guess he didn't like the hole I dug. I thought it was pretty good. I worked my butt off!"

"Let's take a look," he said, walking inside. His mouth dropped open when he saw it. "Holy shit Blizzard! How do you expect anyone to straddle that?"

Holy shit seemed to be the standard reaction to my hole. "Straddle?" I asked.

"Yeah, Blizzard, straddle! You know, to do your business." He could see the wheels turning in my head. I was confused. "A little trench that runs between your feet," he continued to explain, holding his hands about six inches apart. "How do you expect anyone to straddle this monstrosity?"

"Well, I just figured they would drop their drawers, hover over one of the sides, point and shoot. In a crunch, we could line up three men on either side, back to back, and one on each end. That gives us room for eight men at a time. But now that I think about it, your method makes more sense."

"Point and shoot, Blizzard?"

"That's the Army way isn't it, Top?"

He laughed, a little, maybe. "A guy would have to take off his pants to straddle that gorge!"

Both of us looked at the *grave*. In the fresh dirt on one side, was a heavy boot print. On the other side was a heavy footprint, toe indentions included. Both cut a channel in the fresh clay that leads into the hole. It was obvious the colonel had fallen in. We both peered over the edge and could see where his back had left an impression on the soil at the bottom of the pit. Thank God no one else had used it yet.

All I could do now was hope Top could see the humor in it. I looked at him and shrugged my shoulders, "Well apparently the good colonel couldn't wrap his mind around my point-and-shoot method. Looks like he was still trying to do it old school."

He did laugh this time. The top was cool. "Fill in the Grand Canyon Blizzard. Take your shovel and cut a little trench next to it, a shovel wide and a shovel deep. Dumbass. Understood?"

"Yes, First Sergeant," I said and laughed. I was slow, but catching on.

Then I filled and filled. And filled some more. Once the crater was gone, I dug a little trench next to it... in about five minutes. Side note: Straddling is a superior method to point and shoot. Additional side note: Never try to poop into a foxhole. If life ever brings you the opportunity, pass. And if you do, then use the point-and-shoot method. Don't try to straddle it.

# Chapter 14 Steering Wheel Intermonial

If you read no other chapter in this book, please read this one. A good skeptic could easily dismiss any of my Intermonials as flukes, coincidences, or just crazy nature. Not this one.

What happens next could only have been caused by a higher power. Like every word in this book, the next story is true. I carry it with me for comfort. Any time I get discouraged and wonder if God is real, all I have to do is remember what happened that night at Ft. Campbell in 1987. Since then I have KNOWN there is a greater force in the universe. I still have to have FAITH in God to save me, which I do, but in His existence, I have been sure of since the night I called Him out. This is what happened, God's truth.

WARNING: Do not use the following method to see God. Oh, you might meet Him, but you'll die doing it. Relax and just read about it. I did it for you.

## The Mustang

It was sometime during spring (April, I believe), 1987 at Ft. Campbell, KY. A couple of buddies and I were driving down 41A- the main drag that runs in front of the base and separates KY and TN in places. All I remember about that strip is three things; bars, pawn shops and used car dealers. Oh, I'm sure there were others, but I didn't notice them. We were driving past one of those buy-here/pay-here car lots when I saw a sign saying: Mustang $1588. "Stop dude!" I said. "Not that I'm going to buy a car from these shysters, but for that price we might as well take a look at it."

It turned out to be a 1974 Mustang II Ghia. It had a V-6 with dual exhaust and an odometer that read somewhere in the 60,000-mile range. The outside was white and the top was black vinyl. The inside was cheap vinyl/plastic, but I'm telling you true, there was not a rip, tear, or nick anywhere in the upholstery. It was flawless. Even the trunk was the showroom.

*Try–n–Save* wouldn't budge on the price. I didn't blame them. It was a nice car. I signed the papers and drove it off the lot. That's the thing about being in the military; you always have credit. I gave them a copy of my LES (Leave Earnings Statement) and my signature. That's all they needed to ensure they were going to get paid. It didn't matter if I was shipped overseas the next day; they had my LES and my signature. As long as I stayed in the military, it was money in the bank to them. No wonder they let me drive off with only liability insurance on a car that wasn't paid for.

That was Sunday. I drove back to base and called Fatneck in Michigan to tell her about my new ride. Excuse me, our new ride. We were engaged and this was going to be our first car when we got married in January. Then we would move down to Kentucky, where we would stay until I got out of the Army in August. That part of the plan happened... the Mustang didn't make it past Thursday.

I was waxing it after work- a mere four days into ownership when the two buddies I had been with when I bought it walked over. One was John Campbell and the other was a guy named Z.

John Campbell is his real name. John, if you read this please contact me so we can relive that night. I tried to find you on Facebook. I figure if you're not there, you're either dead or in prison. I wish you the best, man. You were a good friend to me during Basic Training.

As for Z... sorry I can't remember your name. I sure remember finding my review mirror the next morning with two big cracks filled with blood and hair. It sure explained how you got the crack in your forehead, anyway. The same goes for you, man. I want to hear from you too so we can relive what happened. I know you remember.

"Hey, Blizz," John, said as they walked up, "How's the new ride?"

"She's sweet!" I said and popped the hood to show off the V-6. Both of these guys had seen it before, but I still liked showing it off. Then, after looking them up and down to make sure their clothes were clean, I invited them to check out the inside.

"Let's take a cruise down to the park," Z said. "We can show off your new ride to the babes."

"Let's get something to drink while we're at it." I insisted. "I'm not going there sober."

"Shotgun!" John said.

# Evercrap Park

The park was along a river in Clarksville, TN. It's where we sometimes hung out on weekends- waxing cars, drinking beer, playing Frisbee, and checking out girls. It was normally a cool place to cruise in Clarksville on Friday or Saturday (Even on Sunday afternoon) but not on a Thursday night. On Thursday nights, probably to this day, that park is dead. There was no one parked but us. A few cars went through, but they all seemed to be looking for someplace better to hang out. I didn't blame them.

There we were three dudes with a fifth of 190-proof *Evercrap* and a jug of *Kool Quench*. Between mixing drinks and passing the bottle, the booze was gone in 20 minutes. I remember being a hog and drinking nearly half the bottle myself.

This is where fog rolls in. If you've ever drunk moonshine, then you know what Evercrap tastes like. If you've ever drunk Evercrap, then you know what moonshine tastes like. If you've ever drank half a fifth in twenty minutes, then you've been really, really drunk. And you know how drunk I was. Well, you know how drunk I was about to become. The booze hadn't fully kicked in yet. That was still minutes away. I hit the key and dropped the slapstick into drive. "This place blows. We're outta here, let's go back to base." I said and gunned it. Oh, and if you've never drunk that much- then you have no idea.

## Guardhouse Road

Since Ft. Campbell is a closed base, you need a decal on the front of your car to be granted access to the post. If the guard at the gate sees the emblem on your bumper, he waves you through. If he doesn't see an emblem, he waves you over to a secondary guard shack to explain yourself to an MP. Since I had just bought the car, I didn't have a decal. And since I was drunk and smelled like Evercrap, I didn't want to talk to an MP. That meant getting on base the back way.

Behind Ft. Campbell there was a two-lane ash fault road that led up to a small (then) two-man operated guard shack. Of note, I have been there recently and it is much, much bigger with lots of guards. I can't see them just waving you through nowadays because you have short hair. Back then, however, the guard would stop us, glance at our military haircuts, and give motion for us to drive on. He always did. By going in the back way, I wouldn't have to answer questions or breathe on anyone.

That was the plan. Then the fog started rolling in. If fog equals drunk, brother, I was in London on one of those nights so thick it gets talked about for years- perhaps generations. But every word I say here is true. Right down to the half-fifth of Evercrap, I drank in twenty minutes, those details are accurate to within one or two ounces and one or two minutes. I remember them so clearly because I relived everything that happened that night many times the next day and so many times since that some things got locked in forever- like 106 miles per hour.

That is how fast a 1974 Mustang II Ghia with a V6 and dual exhaust will go. Well, that's how fast mine went anyway. Through the fog, I can still see the speedometer. It's about all I remember really, but I still see it clearly as Christmas- and the steering wheel. On the edges of my memory I see the centerline of the road racing past but what I see most clearly, is the steering wheel, the dash, and 106 mph. I held it to the mat for eternity, begging for more, but that's as far as the needle would go.

I finally backed off the gas and watched as the needle moved below a hundred. There was a stop sign ahead where 'Route 106' came to a T. I'll call that Guardhouse Road. Since I had a hard left turn coming up, I slowed down to 70 mph.

From what my extremely frightened passengers told me the next day, they were screaming at me to slow down. I do remember screaming, but I honestly don't remember who was doing it or why. That, my friend, is fog. I remember attempting to make my turn and thinking I would end up drifting onto the shoulder of Guardhouse Road; I mean, after all, I was doing seventy mph. But man oh man; I couldn't wait to see the look on John and Z's faces after I made the turn. I knew they were scared. I was too drunk to be scared.

That's what I remember. And that IS what happened. There was more, but I will tell you about that tomorrow. Right now I have an impossible turn ahead. In my mind, it was possible though. Like I said, I knew we would go wide. My mind had that figured right anyway... and I'm right about slowing down to seventy too. That's what the speedometer read the last time I checked anyway. Right before I white knuckled the steering wheel and started my left turn.

# (Intermonial #3)

Just as I started my turn, the steering wheel spun out of my hands. It was like holding onto an engine's flywheel when someone hits the key- it spun that hard and fast. It went counterclockwise the first time. To this day I can tell you the exact words that screamed in my head, verbatim: "NOW, IS NOT THE TIME TO LOSE CONTROL!"

I was scared now. Taking a T intersection at seventy mph didn't scare me, but that wheel ripping out of my hands sure did. I grabbed it again. What else could I do? I had to regain control.

No sooner had I grabbed the wheel and it spun again- this time clockwise, with that same 'flywheel' force. Again my hands flew off. I can't remember what went through my brain at that time, but I'm sure it wouldn't be fit for print even if I could. The only thing I could do was to grab the steering wheel again. And that's what I did.

Thankfully, this time my grip held and the wheel didn't spin. Grass and weeds flew past- I guessed we were in a field. I was steering as best I could and breaking when I looked up in time to see a wall of yellow.

The car nearly came to an instant stop. I'd guess we were still going about fifty mph by the time we hit what turned out to be a sand embankment. The front of the car buckled and we ramped airborne. The car landed and we went down into the ditch of Guardhouse Road. We rocketed out of that, crossed Guardhouse Rd, and went into the ditch on the other side. I steered out of that and I finally regained enough control to bring us to a stop back on the right shoulder of Guardhouse Road.

## Whew, what a ride!

The engine had stalled so I hit the key. Nothing. "Now what's wrong?" I asked God. We got out and stood watching the steam roll out from under the Mustang's hood. No sooner did we step out of the car than a pickup truck stopped. The driver called out through the passenger window, "Did you get him?"

None of us knew what to say. We had no idea what he was talking about. We exchanged puzzled looks and silence. Finally, Z spoke for the confused group and said, "Huh?"

"The deer! The deer! Did you get him?" I realized he must have thought we had hit a deer and was hoping for some fresh road-kill to take home in his truck.

"No, he ran off into the woods," I lied to end the conversation.

"Dammit!" he cursed and drove off. Sorry to ruin your dinner plans buddy.

We popped the hood and saw the grill and radiator were smashed into the fan. Bessie wasn't going anywhere. We walked to the guard shack and told the MP we crashed our car hitting a deer. He smelled the booze and knew all three of us were drunk, but what could he do? He let us walk through. No problem. We walked back to the 3rd Brigade and passed out. No problem.

# The next day...

The next morning the three of us went back to the scene. There was Sally, still sleeping. We looked at her sober this time. She looked even worse than she did the night before. Besides the smashed grill, the entire front clip (hood and fenders) was crushed and the frame twisted. She had to be put down. It was the only humane (financially sensible) thing to do.

We continued walking down to the 70 mph intersection where I had attempted my left turn. And to my credit, I did make the turn. It cost me my car and was scary as hell, but I had what was left of her pointed in the right direction. Mission accomplished there.

We walked down and stood where the car had gone off the road. Well, the first time it went off the road anyway. What we saw will stay with me for the rest of my life. I bet it stayed with John and Z too.

The three of us stood facing the road we turned off from. There were tire tracks that cut two groves into the soft Kentucky bluegrass that went exactly, and Lord I stress EXACTLY, between a telephone pole

Chris Blizzard

and a sinkhole with six inches to spare on either side. The sinkhole was an oval about twelve feet across by twenty feet long and eight feet deep.

To do that maneuver in daylight I would need to creep down that slope, riding the break; hopefully with someone ground guiding me to keep me from dropping my right tire into the sinkhole while I would be focusing on keeping my driver's door from scraping against the telephone pole. I certainly wouldn't try that move at 70 mph. There is no way the maneuver is even possible. Physics simply wouldn't allow for such a thing to happen.

"That's where the steering wheel spun out of my hands," I told John. Z was busy walking around the hole, shaking his head.

"That's when you were calling out God, dude," John said.

"Huh?" I had no idea what he was talking about.

"Yeah man, you were asking us if we believed in Jesus Christ. You don't remember calling out God and the devil?"

"I did that?" I said. It was news to me. Like I said, I remember screaming. I remember the speedometer. And I darn sure remember that steering wheel spinning out of my hands. But I don't remember asking God or Jesus to get involved.

"Blizzard, you were a total madman last night," John said. "You were asking me and Z if we believed in Christ? You were yelling at God and asking Him if He was real. The last thing you said was, "Who's stronger God, you or the devil?' That's when we left the road."

I stood looking at the tracks cut between the telephone pole and the sinkhole. All three of us did. "I guess God must be stronger," Z said.

110

We all agreed.

It's not like the three of us were close friends before that night, but after that night neither one of them talked to me much again. If we passed, they would smile and say hello... and keep walking. I guess one night of partying with the ol' Blizzman was all they could handle. Pansies.

# Intermonial in Review: And that is how I know...

That steering wheel spinning out of my hands is how I KNOW that God is real. My faith... or questioning thereof, brought me that knowledge. That's what I know. And I am quite certain that is THE most important law in the universe. That is the most important thing I want to say in this book; God is real. My other Intermonials may be evidence of it, but this one is proof!

Knowing is different than believing. That steering wheel spinning out of my hands is how I know. All you can do is take my word for it, and I hope you do, but I lived it. I was there. Was I drunk? I wouldn't have done it if I hadn't been, but it happened. Nothing physical could have caused that steering wheel to spin like that. Even if I did hit something in the road, which I didn't, that in your wildest dreams could have caused the tires to move suddenly- hence spinning the wheel out of my hands, that car should have flipped.

It should have... but it didn't. That defied physics. All of my Intermonials, from dismissing Bob calling as bad timing or that bird just being crazy, and other things you will read about- as just getting lucky, can be explained on a non-supernatural level. Not my steering wheel Intermonial. That one is different.

Think about that the next time you're driving along at 70 mph. For the love of God and all His angels don't actually do this, but just think about what would happen if you suddenly spun your steering wheel to the left... or the right. Unless you are on ice, your car will flip like a discarded beer can. It would have to.

For my car to perfectly execute that impossible maneuver between the pole and the sinkhole (with the steering wheel spinning uncontrollably), to me is proof that God exists. I've never questioned His existence since that night. I certainly never called Him out again either. Or got that drunk again. Well, not that I remember anyway.

# PAUSE

It's spring 1987 and the next Intermonial I have for you doesn't happen until December 23, 2005. That's a long time. Will do my best to keep the story moving into my next life-saving Intermonial. You really should stick around for that one... it's a real doozy

# The Second Half...

This story started out to be a testament to some of the things God has done in my life. I've tried to remain true to that objective even though I tossed in a bunch of extra crap; some relevant, some iffy. Unfortunately, the crap tossing will undoubtedly continue since my next Intermonial (to make the book, anyway) doesn't happen until 2005.

A lot happens between those years; about ten more books really. I will try to stay with the things that are relevant to my story, but I'm certain to wander off the reservation from time to time. I have to admit though, it was fun to see those drill sergeants' faces again when I took my socks off. It was a real giggle-kill. It was also good to see Afro-Joe again.

So far I have counted three Intermonials. No doubt there were others, some I may have noticed, most I probably didn't. Those are three that made the book so far. There is another life-and-death one coming. In that one, God reaches down and bails me out again from another death ride.

Towards the end of my tale, now that I am looking for God, Intermonials will happen more often. Not as dramatic as birdbrains or crashes perhaps, but works of God nonetheless. As always, you will be invited to draw your own conclusions as to whether or not they were divine, but you will need to know more about my life to understand what brings me to these points.

# The Roaring

# Twenties

# Chapter 15 My Best Days

Fatneck and I were married in Michigan, on January 23, 1988. I was discharged (honorably) from Ft. Campbell, KY on 18 August 1988. We had two choices on where to move, out west to Arizona or up north to Michigan. It was no contest; we chose sunshine over snow.

Getting out of the Army and moving to Arizona (again, but this time with a wife) divides my life into two halves, the one before kids, and the one after. The wife didn't last. We are good friends nowadays. Even she introduces herself as Fatneck sometimes. Since I'm the one who gave her that little moniker, you can safely assume virtually every problem in our marriage was my fault. Normally I don't feel comfortable speaking for someone else, but on this count, I am quite certain Fatneck would wholly concur with that. There are some names I'm simply keeping disguised; such as her new husband, Number Two; Or as I like to call him in homage to his Mexican heritage, Numero Dos.

UPDATE: He is now another ex-husband, and I'm still not putting him in here.

They had two children together, but before Dos came along, we had two of our own. We started with Jacob Ryan, in November 1990, followed by Jared Taylor, in February 1993. We split when the boys were two and four years old; the reasons for our breakup, along with why I got custody of our children instead of her, do not belong in this book. In the interest of keeping some things private and the story moving, I will advance to my life as a single, full-time dad. Good times.

This picture was taken shortly after my split from Fatneck. Good times.

# 26<sup>th</sup> Place

When the ex and I split, we were renting a two-bedroom house on 26<sup>th</sup> Place. Again, skipping over our personal issues as much as possible let me just say that I moved out and left her with the kids... and some of her friends, including Dos.

I went to live with a friend, Tom, on the north side of town who was recently divorced. Every morning- even though FN wasn't working, I picked up the boys and took them to daycare (at a cost of $700/month, hem). Then, after working all day, I would pick the kids up, drive back to 26th Place, drop them off with Fatneck and her crew, and then go back to Tom's for the night. That routine went on for about two months... until Dawn (the owner of the rental house) evicted FN and her group of homeboys for not paying rent. I moved back in, cleaned the place up, and paid the back rent. After that, I got to stay home with my boys at night instead of going to Tom's house.

What is notable here is how I fixed and saved my life and home. Whenever my life has needed fixing, I've always fixed it. Whenever my life has been good, eventually, I've always torn it down. Maybe I've done that so things would need fixing again? At any rate, this was a time in my life when I was building and tending things. These were my best days. I even got a dog.

My neighbor, Louise, found a stray and asked me if I could keep him fenced in my backyard for the night until she could take him to the dog pound in the morning. I agreed, happy to help a neighbor. I met her out front to collect the mutt.

# I got Moxie

I can still see that golden retriever dancing around Louise's feet. She waved at me and said, "Here he is. He's kinda wild."

"Come here, boy!" I said, crouching down. He heard my voice, turned his head, and came bounding at me headlong. He ran into my arms, about knocked me over, and started licking me. At first, I fell back, regained my balance, and hugged him. When I stood up, he stood on his hind legs so he could be part of the conversation. It was a move Moxie would repeat a lot over the years, in his younger years anyway.

"Yeah Chris, if you could keep him in your yard overnight, that would be great. Those kids," she said, lowering her voice and pointing at the house across the street where poor grandma, bless her heart, was trying to raise three delinquents that her daughter had dumped on her. "Those kids couldn't take care of a pet rock," she said. "When I saw them come home with this dog, I ran right over there and made them give it to me before they killed it. You know my dog is so mean I can't keep him at my place. I'll take him to the pound in the morning. He'll be gone before you go to work."

"Sounds good Louise. He doesn't look like he'll be much trouble. What's his name?"

"He doesn't have one. Thanks again, Chris."

We said our goodnights and I looked down at a block-headed golden retriever with a large black tear birthmark in the center of his tongue. "OK dog, follow me." We walked into the backyard and I gave him a rough tour, introducing him to the storage shed, the tangerine tree, and the side yard, off the dining room. He peed on all of them. I set him out a bowl of water and went into the dining room to sit down and watch him. He walked around the yard smelling and peeing. After he was done with that he came over to the dining room door and lay down.

With his yellow mane, he seemed like a lion looking over his kingdom. I went back outside and played with him. We did that for a while; then I went back inside the house, and he followed.

I was getting a little too attached to a dog that would be gone in the morning so I put him back outside. I sat down at the kitchen table and watched as he lay against the door again and returned to surveying his domain. He was panting to stay cool- Moxie always panted, but he also seemed to be smiling. I called Louise and told her not to take him to the pound in the morning. That dog was home.

"What are you going to name him?" She asked.

"I still don't know. I'll get back to you on that," I said. "For now, leave my dog alone."

She laughed and wished us well. As I hung up I realized I had been playing with the whole, 'watch this dog overnight until I can take him to the pound in the morning', routine. Good one, Louise, well played.

She did ask a good question: What's his name? When I looked at him I thought of Old Yeller. That was my favorite story as a kid. My poor brother Aaron, bless his heart, read that to me a million times. He would ask me if I wanted to hear any of the other tales from my big book of kid's stories... but I never did. A few of those were dog stories too, but the only one I cared about was Old Yeller. Now I had an Old Yeller of my very own.

Old Yeller was too common of a name though. Sure he reminded me of Old Yeller, but he wasn't. He was my dog. And Old Yeller's story didn't end well. I remembered a bricklayer who did some work to the Crab's cabin on Lynx Lake. He had an old yellow pickup truck with the words 'Old Yeller' written in black letters on the bed. It seemed to me that the guy had a really cool name, but I couldn't remember what it was.

Then it came to me... "Moxie!" That old guy's name was Moxie. I opened the door and said, "Get in here Moxie. You're sleeping with me!"

I gave him a bath his first night. It was a risky move, but I filled the tub halfway up and set him in. I used a big cup to wash and rinse. He wasn't happy about it, but he behaved well. I guessed him to be about one year old, and since he didn't understand basic commands, I also figured that he had been neglected most of his young life. That all changed the night he found the Blizzard home.

Fatneck dropped the kids back at home the day after I got Moxie. Since I wanted the boys to be surprised, I told her beforehand- under the strictest confidence, that I had a dog for the kids. She promised she wouldn't tell them about it so it would be a surprise when she brought them home.

When she showed up, I left Moxie in the living room and kept the door closed so the kids couldn't see their new dog. The first thing Ryan said after getting out of the car was, "Where's the dog?"

"I thought we had an agreement," I said, glaring at FN.

"I didn't tell them!" she said, indignantly.

"Mom told us Dad you had a surprise. She said you couldn't tell us what it was, but it has four legs and a tail. I guess she thinks we're pretty stupid, huh? I hope it's not a cat. Where's my dog?"

That was Ryan. From the time he learned to talk to this day, he gets straight to the point. I opened the front door and let Moxie out. Moxie wiggled around and licked the boys like long-lost friends. He went into his trademark standing dance and put his arms on the boy's shoulders. He danced around until one of them hugged him. Then he hugged them back and licked them. It was a good meeting, even if it wasn't a surprise.

Ryan and Moxie the day they met. I sure miss that dog.

## Movin' On Over

The next major life change came about six months later when my next-door neighbor, Larry, told me he was defaulting on his mortgage and his house was going back to the owner. Long story short, I found the owner and offered him $48,000. He accepted and with my Veteran's home loan, I was able to move in with no money down.

Since the house was right next to the one I was renting, I simply took down a section of wooden fence that divided the two properties and spent the next month moving next door, one armload at a time. My new house had only one bedroom, but it was plenty big enough for the three of us. Excuse me, the four of us. God bless Moxie; that dog followed me everywhere. I was the center of his world. And just like Blanca, I never had to worry about him running away. Moxie always stayed close to home. If I did accidentally leave him on the outside of the fence, I would usually find him sitting by the front door, smiling, waiting to be let back inside.

In the backyard of my tiny house was an even tinier guesthouse. My house was built in 1948 and the guesthouse was added sometime during the '70s. In order to comply with city building codes, it was built without a kitchen. I added that on so I could rent it out. I used the extra income from that to help pay for toys and fun.

For toys, I had a Suburban, a bass boat, golf clubs, shotguns and rifles, bows and arrows. Most weekends I went out to play while the boys went to their mom's, but on the weekends I kept them, the boys, Moxie and I went fishing, hunting, golfing... whatever. Us Blizzard boys were always doing something fun. I remembered how much I loved the outdoors growing up so I figured my kids would too. They did. And they loved '70s music... bless their hearts.

Looking back, raising my kids on 26th Place was the best time of my life. Then came Internet dating... and Attila. Again, the name! I'm so stupid.

The boys and our house on 26th Place in Phoenix. My best days. So far anyway.

# Chapter 16 Attila

Again, the name. Why didn't I take that as a bad sign? There were so many red flags. I wish I were smarter. It's not easy going back to that time in my life. We won't stay there long, I promise. I just want to show you what marks the end of the *good ol' days* for the Blizzard boys. It ended the longest streak I had gone without tearing my life down.

The year the boys and I lived with Attila and her three Huns was the second hardest time in my life. Not because of the Huns, mind you, her kids were adorable, but Attila and I were simply a mismatch. We had gotten together twice, once at her house and once at mine. We never went on any actual dates. It was obvious (to me anyway) that weren't a good match. I was ready to break it off with her when I got *The Call*.

## The Crash

It was Attila. She had been in a car accident. Her neck and back were badly hurt and her car was totaled. Long story short (and I do want to keep this part short; as I don't like revisiting this time in my life), she was too banged up to work. She was now a single mom with three kids, no job, and no car.

## What I Should Have Said

What was I supposed to tell her? "Gee I'm sorry you're having such a bad day, BUT I don't want to see you anymore. We both need to move on. Good luck with everything. Remember, I'm not breaking up with you because your life has taken such a devastating turn; I'm breaking up with you because I don't like you. Honest."

# What I Said

I'm just not that cold. I should have been. Sure, I would have said it a lot nicer than that, but I should have said it. Instead, as someone who has a natural impulse to help others, this is closer to what I actually said, "You poor thing. As soon as I get out of work, I'll pick up the boys and come right over to make dinner for you and the kids. Hang on. I'll be there soon."

# End of a Good Run

I didn't know it, but I had just made the first in a long line of terrible choices. It was like the bird all over again. Only this time I had a whole flock of them chasing me down, dropping poop bombs. But you know me; I kept trudging along, doing what I could, afraid to hurt someone's feelings.

She had smashed her car and was laid up with three kids, a house payment, and no job. Instead of thinking with my head and going through with breaking up with her, I thought with my heart and went to help her. Within a couple of weeks, I was spending every night at her house and my kids were staying with her during the day to save on daycare expenses. Eventually, I moved them into her school system and rented out my house on 26<sup>th</sup> Place. What was I thinking?

I had gotten used to dealing with just me and the boys for so long, that I wasn't ready for someone else's issues; least of all Attila's. And when I say issues, brother, I'm talking major childhood stuff. I can honestly say ninety percent of our problems were her fault. She had a rough upbringing, to be sure (Raped by her brother since she was three years old, etc.), but she wanted (and expected) me to pay for every wrong that was ever done to her. That was I debt I didn't owe and one I couldn't afford to pay. But God helped me, I tried to pay for it. I started paying on that tab from the day I moved in with her.

A typical morning- and by typical I mean almost every single blessed morning, began with her sending me off to work with at least one nasty remark, just to make sure I wasn't happy; and most days a slew of them. "Don't get sidetracked on your way home after work. I know you're going by your old house to collect rent. That shouldn't take long. Make sure you call me when you leave so I know what time to expect you. The washing machine is acting up again, but don't worry about it. I will just deal with it after I finish getting all these kids off to school. Oh, but you just go have a relaxing day at work where you don't have to deal with any of this. And tell that bank teller, the one I know you think is so hot, that I said, hi!"

The evenings were worse. Much worse. That's when she got ugly. After all, she had an entire day of misery and drinking to unload by the time I got home from work. Most nights I drove home hoping to God she wouldn't be waiting to pounce on me when I walked in the door. Many times I asked Jesus Himself to bring that woman peace; at least enough so we wouldn't end the night in a fight. However, most of those prayers went unanswered.

As with my marriage, I won't go into our troubles, but I will say that we drank too much. Most days I started drinking from the time I got home from work until she got tired of yelling at me and fell asleep. Even as I walked through that hell, I knew God and Jesus were watching over me. I wonder if they saw my situation as I see it now, *the beginning of another demise for Chris Blizzard*. Of course, they had to watch my kids go through it with me. Only the good Lord knows how many nights our five kids lay in their beds, listening to us yell at each other.

I guess there wasn't much God or Jesus could do but shake their heads. I don't know why I moved in with Attila. I guess a lot of it had to do with her kids. They were precious, and a great fit with mine. It was a tough year for certain, but it wasn't all bad. The kids were the good part. She had one boy and two girls. Her son was the oldest of her three and was in fourth grade, while my boys were in third and fifth. If memory serves, her daughters were in second grade and kindergarten. We were a family for a year.

# The Huns

I admit it was fun to suddenly have two daughters. One day after work I was standing in her kitchen when her youngest brought me a picture she had drawn that day in kindergarten. It was a typical kid's whale; a figure eight with a tail, mouth, and eye. It had a star at the top and she was quite proud of it.

"Look what I drew at school, Bwizzy," she said handing it to me, awaiting my approval.

I smiled at it and said reflectively, "Ah, Moby Dick."

She snatched it out of my hands and glared at me, becoming a mini-Attila, and said, "It's not a dick. It's a whale!" Then stormed off to her bedroom as I tried to explain (between laughs) what I meant.

One time we went camping in the mountains of Northern Arizona. Our kids went exploring together, fished, played in the fire, and learned to throw knives, as a family. Well, the boys learned to throw knives anyway. The girls went off to do whatever it is girls do when they're camping.

I thought her son, *Rufus*, was in a tough situation. He had two little sisters and was being raised by a single mom. He saw his dad most weekends, but when they did something together, it was an activity that made the girls happy too. His young, impressionable life revolved around chicks. The poor boy was begging to do man-stuff.

Now he had two brothers. They could teach him everything from how to tie on a fishhook to shoot a gun... safely. Side note: I always emphasized safety and no one getting hurt, even though we did sometimes. Hey, such is a boy's life. But even back in early grade school my boys were shooting real guns with dad and carrying BB guns alone. Hey, they never shot each other- so they did better than me.

Rufus loved boy stuff too. He sure took to knife throwing. As I recall, he had a natural feel for it. Yes, technically, letting kids throw knives may be a little dangerous, but so what? It was also dangerous to raise a boy around nothing but girls. The Blizzard family was all boys. If Ryan and Jared had had a sister, that poor girl would have grown up butch as a switchblade.

But back to my three sons... I set up a throwing station in front of a fat, soft tree and grooved a firing line in the dirt with the heel of my boot.

I set it the right distance for a knife to tumble one and a half times before sticking into the tree; that was providing you had a smooth release of the blade.

"Too much *flippy, flippy* and it won't hit tip-first," I explained. Then I threw the knife that way so it bounced off the tree, flying back a couple of feet towards us. "That's why everyone must be behind the firing line when someone is throwing. On a hard throw, the knife can come all the way back to where you're standing... so if you're standing next to the guy that's throwing, pay attention! And if it flies back, don't try to catch it. Just let it land on the ground. Any questions? No? Good. Here's my knife. Don't lose it. I'll be at camp if you need me. Be careful boys."

With the basics out of the way, I walked back to our campsite (about 100 yards away) and had a beer. I was sitting in my lawn chair, listening to nature, when The Storm rolled in. "DO YOU KNOW WHAT THOSE KIDS ARE DOING?" Attila thundered.

"They're supposed to be throwing my knife into a tree," I said. "They're not playing catch with it, are they?"

The girls laughed. Attila didn't.

Now that I think about it... that WAS a brief good time. From there the conversation descended... as most of them did. Not all her fault, not all mine. We were simply oil and water. The drinking didn't help our problems, but yeah, I blame her for most of our misery.

As much as I like seeing the kids again, I need to keep moving. Without trying to explain a relationship that I don't understand myself. Let me just say the boys and I loaded up the burb and the boat with everything we brought and left her house in one haul. As we drove off, I felt the weight of the world lift off my shoulders. The kids and I all agreed how happy we were to be leaving. Again, God only knows why I went there in the first place, but I'm not sure even He knows why I stayed so long. But after a final showdown with Attila, I moved my kids and me back home.

## The Decent Continues

A year after moving in with her and at the end of our relationship- of all times, I quit my job at The Print Shop I had worked at for twelve years, to take a job at Roy's Print shop on Attila's side of town. Roy laid me off five weeks later, while I was in the process of moving the kids and me back to 26th Place.

The front house was rented out, but I had just evicted No-pay Sue from the guesthouse. It was tiny, but the kids and I were back home. Only now I was unemployed. Since I hadn't been at my new job for ninety days, I didn't qualify for unemployment benefits. The $600/month rent from my front house was my only income. I had gone from living in the 'big' house (now 900 sq. ft. seemed like a big house) and holding the same job for over a decade, to being unemployed and living in a 200 sq. ft. guesthouse, with a broken AC, that No-pay Sue had left filthy- on a gross and disgusting level.

## What I Should Have Done

In hindsight, I should have found another job. I could have let my renters in the front house finish their lease and then moved me and the kids back up front. I could have rented the guesthouse back out and

returned to how life was, without my old job, but wiser. Wouldda...
couldda... shouldda... but didn't.


# What I Done

It was during the height of the real estate boom when home values were
soaring. The house I had bought for $48,000 was now in a
neighborhood where some were selling over $200,000. By now I was
so used to making bad decisions- and since I've never been very bright
to begin with, I finally realized the problem, Arizona.

I went to the bank and borrowed about $30,000 (or so?) to fix up my
house. Among my bazillion projects, I added two bedrooms to the main
house and had it painted and re-carpeted. I also had new stucco put on
the house and guesthouse. Another long story short, when I was all
done fixing it up, I sold it for appx. $140,000.


# A Guys Trip

Since I was a groomsman for Buford Crab, our arrival back in
Michigan coincided with his wedding date. If memory serves, that was
November 1, 2002. I'm guessing the year, but that sounds right. During
my house remodel, I paused to take the boys and me to Texas for a fly-
fishing trip that was designated a 'bachelor's weekend' for Buford.

In attendance at the fishing lodge were Buford, Jim, and Jim's father,
*Will*. Also on the trip were John- Buford's soon-to-be father-in-law and
Mike- Buford's Best Man. That made a total of six guys send a
condemned brother to the gallows over a long weekend. Basically, we

sat around a picnic table for three days getting drunk. Will, a non-drinker, fished a little, but Jim, Buford, Mike, and John pretty much just sat there for three days drinking from early in the morning until late at night.

Well, not me. If it was light outside, I was fishing. Oh, I drank my share and even took beer down to the river with me on occasion, but true to Chris Blizzard form, I fished every chance I could. I didn't fly-fish though; I used my bass rod and reel. I out-fished everyone too, the guides and their clients included. On my first morning, I caught fourteen basses before breakfast. When I was in the dining room giving my account, I was greeted with sneers and jeers. No one believed me. Well, every word in this book is true and I caught fourteen bass that morning before breakfast... and a lot more after. That's also true. ☺

Occasionally one of the other guys in my group would wade out into the stream to cast one of their expensive fly rods, but mostly they just sat there and drank. Jim's dad, an elderly man, didn't drink much. Age may have kept him from making many treks down to the water, but *The Drink* held the rest back. Their high-dollar fly rods looked quite impressive, leaning against the wooden fence. Will, a non-drinker used his rod, but Jim, Mike, John, and Buford's rods pretty much just sat there for three days, looking like a picture from a fly fishing catalog.

# Texas Priest

Between the time I ran away from his home back in 1985 and today, Jim Crab became Father Jim Crab and went on to open his own Charismatic, catholic church. Although I'm still unclear exactly how a priest can be married, it has something to do with the word 'charismatic' and his church not being endorsed by the Roman Catholic (with an uppercase C) church. At any rate, he has a small church on his property in Texas and holds mass every Sunday.

In high school, we only went to church for funerals or weddings. Now that he was a priest, he went to church every Sunday, but to me, he was still the same guy. He drank like the same guy; that didn't change. He still treated Lulu like an interruption. And he can hardly get through a conversation without taking the Lord's name in vain.

It is not the intention of this book to embarrass anyone. Many names have been changed, including Jim, Buford, and Will's. I would also like to add that Jim's' dad, is one of the finest men I've ever met. Jim is like his father in many ways but falls far short in many others. Again I don't wish to disparage anyone and truly my accounts are selective. For instance, I don't mean to portray Jim as someone who drinks every day; he doesn't. Most days he doesn't touch the stuff. Ever since I've known him, from high school through today, he has always been able to stop drinking when the party's over. That was one of his talents I could never master. He could stop after Sunday night. Me? I woke up Monday morning and went looking for another drink.

Let me also reiterate that this story is but a snapshot of my life. If I included everything, this book would never end. As far as God plays into these years, let me summarize that by saying I always saw Him at work in my life- by either keeping me out of relationships or getting

133

me into them; guy friends included. I really have given God credit for most people I have met and the things that have happened in my life since Eagle Boy's Village. But there simply aren't enough pages in this book to tell all my stories. For now, for some inexplicable reason, I have to sell my wonderful little house in paradise and move BACK to Michigan. Aye! Aye! Aye!

# Chapter 17 Hello Michigan Hello Beer

"Hello, Mike." He was a schoolmate from my Hemlock days. He had been a grade behind me in school and was the Best Man in Buford's upcoming wedding. He let my kids, Moxie and Sparky (The Laughing Dog), and I live with him at his house in *Draginaw*, Michigan no questions asked. As a matter of fact, he welcomed us with open arms. God bless him. We showed up with our Suburban, pulling the bass boat; heaped and stuffed with everything we owned.

"Hey Blizz," he said when we pulled up. "Beer?"

"I thought you'd never ask," I said.

So my alcoholism grew beyond Phoenix. The big difference now was that I had a fat bank account and no house to remodel or pesky job to interfere with my drinking. It didn't take long before I would start drinking beer most days right after I got home from taking the boys to school. By the time they got home that afternoon, I was usually both half drunk and happy to see them, or I had just slept off my morning buzz and was working on another.

## Ripe for the Picking

It made me the perfect find for Arthur. That is his real nickname- that he got from the drunk of movie fame. Again, the name! That time it was a nickname I didn't make up. That time I really should have seen the trouble coming and stepped aside. Since I didn't, I blame the booze. Well, that and I'm not very bright. Sober, I may have seen all the potholes, red signs, and warning flares that were all around me. But loaded with cash and drunk every day (just like in the movie Arthur), I was poised to lose it all. Some days I really wish the good Lord had made me smarter.

Instead of looking at where my life was and assessing my situation realistically, however, I had another beer. And another. As a matter of fact, I was drinking in Mike's garage the morning I met Arthur. That's when he mentioned his "plan" to start a concrete company. He said he had worked for other concrete companies and that making money pouring concrete was a veritable guarantee during the construction boom. It was a combination of him talking a good talk and me listening and drinking; that I heard what I wanted to hear.

To his credit, Mike said that he would never go into business with Arthur. He tried to warn me. I didn't listen to him though. I even ended up using MY money (in our 50/50 partnership) to pay for the incorporation of Blizzard/Scumbag Inc. I used my good name (I still had good credit then) to buy a brand new skid-steer; which is a little four-wheeled earthmover. Yeah, that was another $400/month bill I didn't mind signing for. I was certainly getting tired of spending a couple hundred dollars every time we had to rent one to grade dirt. I even paid to have our business cards printed. I passed those things out to every bar-hag in Draginaw too. I was buying drinks, hob-knobbing, and believing I was King Krap of the business world. When I moved back to Michigan the last time, back in 1986, I was driving a broken-down Pontiac and dead broke. This time I had a three-year-old Suburban, a bass boat, two kids, two dogs, and lots of money. Now I even own a concrete company. Sure, I hadn't poured a lick of mud at that point, but that's on account of it being winter in Michigan. When the ice lifted, we were going to be swamped with work. We were going to be rich. Arthur said so.

We (which means I) rented an unheated space in an old, crumbly sawmill in old town Draginaw. It was a ridiculous place to rent, but we got it through one of Arthur's buddies and I just went along- with a brain only another alcoholic could truly appreciate. I trusted Arthur's judgment. He appreciated my money.

Most days our routine had us down at the sawmill, playing drinking games in front of a large gas-powered space heater. We did that until it was time to hit the local diner where construction people hung out. We would tell anyone who cared (almost no one did) that we had a concrete company down the street and were ready to pour mud. You know, in the spring.

# Poor Time

When spring did come... we poured about half a dozen slabs. To make money, however, we needed to pour about a hundred more. Without getting into all the nuances of the business, let me just say the ground needs to be dry and unfrozen to pour concrete. That spring in Michigan, we never went more than two days without rain. We landed a job pouring a sidewalk through part of a housing development that we never even broke ground on. If we had two days of sunshine, on the third day, the rain came down in buckets and re-soaked the soil. It was so wet we couldn't even level the sod with the skid steer to get ready to pour concrete.

I didn't mention that to the bank when I went for a mortgage though. After a few months of living with Mike, I found a house on 3 acres in Hemlock. We moved in and I enrolled my kids in the same school I had graduated from when I lived with the Crab family. The same school that elected me class partier in 1985. If I had still been in school, I'm confident I would have won that title again. No change there.

The change was drinking at bars. Don't get me wrong; I was never a stranger to the barroom. But in seventeen years of living in Phoenix, I probably went to the bar twenty times or so. Maybe less. In Michigan, though, it got to a point that I went to the bar every day.

Well, nearly every day. Even on days I didn't go to the bar, I would end up drinking. Not necessarily getting drunk, but drinking. Even at places like the *Point And Shoot* gun club. My buddies and I would walk the clay pigeon course passing the flask and blasting our shotguns. I wouldn't drink if I took the boys (they each had their own shotguns, Ryan a twelve gage, Jared a twenty gage and both were crackerjack shots, but most likely I went to the bar when we finished shooting. I'm sorry to say that. I'm ashamed to say that, but that's what I did.

# Proud Poppa

Instead of visiting the bar though, I'd rather go back to the boys' school. They had been transplanted into the country from the city. Each had plenty of girlfriends and both played football. They were the new kids in a community where most people had known each other since kindergarten. In short, they were stars.

One day at a football game when I was standing next to the fence around the field with some other dads. Suddenly a runner from the visiting team broke away after a kick-off... there was simply no way to stop this kid from making a touchdown. Most of the players following him even broke pursuit when it became obvious he couldn't be stopped. In twenty yards he would be in the end zone. Play over.

Not so fast...

Ryan, the Ever-Pursuing Terminator, came up from the side and behind. Suddenly the play was not over. The other dads and I go from scoffing at the inevitable touchdown to cheering a tackle. "Get him! Get him!" we begin yelling. Sure enough, Ryan tackled him at the six-yard line. Side note: They didn't even get a field goal out of the play. "Did you see that? Who is that kid?"

"That's my boy," I said.

"Where did he come from? What's his name? What's your name?" etc. It was a good day.

There should have been a lot more days like that. There would have been too, if it weren't for that damn monkey on my back. When the game was over, I took the kids out to McDonald's, drove them home, and went to the *Swill Pit*. It's what I did most every day back then. I sat around an old country bar with a bunch of other drunks. Man, we must have looked like something; a bunch of guys (and a few hags) sitting around, each with a monkey on their back, demanding another drink.

Dammit! I'm back at the bar again, huh? That's probably where I was when the boys were playing in the snow down our country road the day Jared decided to have some fun. He put his tongue to a stop sign and pretended it was stuck to the frozen surface. The rest of the kids hid while he frantically waved his arms at a passing car. He asked the frightened husband and wife who stopped if they would pour water on it. They didn't have any, but ran to someone's house and borrowed a cup. When they came back, water in hand; ready to free the poor boy (lucky they happened by when they did). Jared pulled his tongue off the sign and said, "Ha! Jokes on you!" Then he ran off laughing with the other kids.

I wasn't there for that one, but I sure wish I were. As an adult I know should tell him how awful that was... to make fun of someone who is trying to help them, for shame. But I was laughing so hard when the kids told me that one; I doubt they would have taken me seriously if I had. Gee, I wonder where my kids get their mischievous side. Must be Fatneck.

# Plastered Poppa

But back to the bar... In Michigan, I got my first (and only) DUI. And I spent my first (but not last) night in jail. When I ran through my money, my Suburban was repossessed. I was back working at a print shop when Doc gave me a 1969 Volvo station wagon so I could get to work. God bless him. I also bought a 1980 Honda 400 motorcycle. It was a cold, wet ride, but it got me to work and the bar. I could write a very sad book on all the hell I put myself through the year and a half we lived in Michigan. I put us all through hell; the boys and dogs included.

If you understand how deep an alcoholic can sink, you may empathize with what I am about to tell you. If not, then you'll probably think I'm an absolute lowlife. Whether I am now or not, I certainly was back then. This story will summarize just how bad off I was. Here's how Sparky, the Laughing Dog, died.

# Pay Cut

I still had the Burb, its payments and I was dead broke to prove it. I was working at a print shop in Midland for twelve dollars an hour. "But back in Arizona, I made nearly twenty dollars an hour!" I argued.

"In Michigan, running a press pays twelve bucks an hour. If you don't want the job, there are a hundred others in line who do."

I took the job. And put my house up for sale. It was time to leave Michigan- again; too bad, the kids loved it. We had a nice house in the country with over 100 blueberry bushes; two horse stalls with a corral, and a detached 2 ½ car garage that had a study built into it. We had lots of great neighbors. I bought a riding lawnmower- on credit, of course. The boys loved to mow the corral. Sometimes, mostly on purpose, they would bog the rider down in a mud rut. Then we would have to pull it out with the skid steer. And, yeah, they learned to operate that too. In short, they became country boys- happy country boys.

I had my dream house. We had a dream life. Sure I was only making twelve bucks an hour, but I could have delivered pizza at night or on weekends, part-time. Blizzard Monkey Brains Inc. had been a money-busting failure. I had lost everything with that concrete business. Or so I thought anyway. But what had I really lost other than a fat bank account and a decent credit rating?

I did you wrong, but at one point the boys and I were living in the guesthouse, with a broken air conditioner, in Phoenix. I was dead broke and unemployed. That's when I first borrowed the money to get my house ready for sale and began this whole adventure in the first place. From that point to this, I had brought us to a veritable paradise. And even with the crappy wages and crappier weather, at least I had a job.

Dammit, I had everything! Just like I did when I was eighteen. And once again I was throwing it all away... over alcohol. That's my story and I'm stuck with it.

Sorry for getting sidetracked with my demise. There's more God coming. I'd like to stay in Michigan a while longer. Maybe go turkey hunting again with the boys. There were so many good times. It wasn't all drinking. I'm just focusing on the drinking because that's what brought me down. It's going to bring me down a lot further in Arizona. And God is going to bail me out again, like He did with that steering wheel... for some reason.

I'll jump ahead to the move back to Arizona. Let me just say I sold our little cottage and walked away with about $5,000. I bought a van to replace my repossessed Suburban. I hired a trucking company to haul my skid steer back to Arizona. That way I could haul the skid steer trailer back to Arizona, loaded up with everything we owned... like the boat had been when we arrived. Of course, I had sold the boat many, many beers ago.

Side note: It was a great boat too! For the guys... and super cool chicks (you know who you are) it was a fiberglass seventeen-foot, fish and ski. It had a 120-hp Johnson outboard that ran so smoothly you could troll all day in the Arizona heat without fouling the plugs. It was an open bow with a foot-controlled trolling motor and fish finder. For protection from the Arizona sun, it had a white canvas Bimini top. The boat was red and white, garage was kept super clean. I had very few problems and the ones it did have were minor. I owned the boat, but the skid steer cost me $470/month. The boat meant fun. The skid steer meant work. I definitely traded down. I digress. Back to the move...

# Chapter 18 Hello Again Arizona Hello Again Beer

When we got back to Arizona in the spring of 2004, my life digressed even further than it did in Michigan. Once again, I crossed the country looking for a better life; when I had it right in front of me. I didn't know I was my own worst problem. I had no idea that I was trying to run away from myself. I can't speak for the rest of the world, but as for me, that plan never worked. I had all my issues waiting for me every time I got to where I was going. Despite being tightly packed into that van, I still made room for my drinking monkey. By now he was a gorilla; yet somehow I squeezed him in. I guess I figured he'd run off at one of the truck stops along the way. He didn't.

We moved in with Bula, Fatneck's mom, and I enrolled the kids in school. I've known her since high school and she was a sweet lady who turned into a great mother-in-law. For many years she was even a great ex-mother-in-law. Through my divorce from her daughter back in the early '90s, we stayed close. After all, I was the one raising her grandchildren. The boys and I went to her house every holiday for family dinners and some weekends just to cook out and go swimming. Bula and I were always tight. She used to say her oldest boy would tease her that I was her favorite son. I might not have been that, but we certainly had a good mother/son bond, that is certain. Well, we did right up until my motorcycle crash. It changed after that. A lot of things changed- me no longer calling her 'ma' for one. We'll get there soon enough. I just have a little more digressing to do. Okay, a lot more, but I will try to keep the story moving.

We lived with her for about two months. Then I found us a fancy *schmancy* apartment in North Scottsdale. I say fancy schmancy only because it was about $300/month more than I would normally spend on rent. I didn't worry about the cost though. I wanted to get the kids in a nice school. Leaving Hemlock had been tough on them. Putting them in a good school was my way of trying to atone for taking them away from a home they loved. I was employed back at the same print shop I had been working at when I met Attila. I wasn't the lead pressman anymore; now I was doing bindery and deliveries... but I was making enough money to afford our new digs.

I couldn't afford the fancy schmancy bar across the street though. When we lived with Bula I took a break from bar hopping. After we moved into our new apartment though, I found a bar I could walk to (no risk of DUI there) that was full of cute chicks- instead of old farmers. I fell right back into my bar rut.

Please don't think all I did was go to work, come home and get drunk. I may make it sound like that, but there has always been a lot more going on with me than just drinking. This just happened to be when I was at my worst in that battle. The troops were taking heavy losses and the enemy was winning. But like I said, we Blizzards are hard workers. After work, I was trying to start a side business with my skid steer. One day I opened up the phone book and just started cold calling construction companies. I asked them if they had any need for a skid steer with an operator. Many of them did, so I was also doing that after work or on weekends, and raising kids- not just drinking.

As far as my skid steer business adventure went, I had two big problems. One, my van was dying. The engine was old and it wanted to overheat in Arizona whenever I towed with it. Two, I simply wasn't a good enough skid steer operator. I may have been good enough to level ground to pour concrete on back in Michigan, but I wasn't good enough to grade twenty yards of sand into multiple tiers for custom homes in Arizona. That job required someone with several years of experience. Now if they needed me to pull a lawnmower out of the mud, I was qualified to do that, but there wasn't any of that work.

Fast-forward about nine months into our next 'new' life. I'm guessing around September 16, 2005... if I remember the date correctly from the arrest report. By this time I had sold the van and filed for bankruptcy. I was down to a piece of crap car that wouldn't pass emissions and my Honda 400 motorcycle that I had bought in Michigan. I rented the skid steer out to a guy who owned a concrete company (one that actually made money) so my monthly payment was covered with a little left over... for beer.

Speaking of beer, I had been 86'd from the fancy schmancy bar across the street from my apartment for being an obnoxious drunk. That meant I had to drive to drink. I was at a bar somewhere in downtown Scottsdale the night Ryan called. It was a Friday night and he was grounded for not doing his chores. He was going through a phase where he simply refused to pick up after himself. If he took a shower, he threw his towel on the floor. If I asked him to pick it up, he wouldn't. If I told him to pick it up, he'd say, "In a minute." The next time I looked, the towel would still be there.

"Ryan, pick up the damn towel!"

"I will! In a minute."

Lately, I have been in phone conferences with his teachers about him not doing his homework. Looking back now I see how all of the problems he was going through were directly related to my drinking. He was a sixteen-year-old kid with an angry drunk for a dad. And the kid had behavior issues? Surprise! Surprise!

But doing the best I could, I'd sit him down and talk until I couldn't stand the sound of my own voice. Five minutes later I'd ask him to take out the trash and the whole scene would start over. It was driving me crazy. So I grounded him, got on my motorcycle... and went to the bar.

At this point in my alcoholism, I was a shell of my former self. I used to be a good dad. This wasn't how I had raised my boys. To be more accurate, this wasn't how I raised my boys before I moved in with Attila. That's when I became a drunk. Don't get me wrong; I don't blame her for my troubles. I don't blame anyone for my problems but me. That is just when my drinking turned daily. I changed from one or two beers after work, into a six-pack or more after work- and all day on weekends- kind of guy.

By September 2005, I was just going through the motions of being a dad. I had my fatherly duties so ingrained through all the years I had actually done it right, that combined with my print and skid steer work, I thought I was doing okay. I was talking to their teachers when something was wrong. Then I'd go home and yell at whichever offender caused the teacher to call me at work in the first place. And God forgive me, even on nights I didn't go to the bar, I drank between nine and twelve beers before bed.

The store, on my way home from work, had eighteen packs for $9.99. I knew I could skip buying beer on my way home if I bought it the day before. Yeah, I could squeeze two nights of drinking out of one eighteen-pack. That became my cycle. May God forgive me.

As I'm about to show you, God darn sure told me to quit. Yes, He did. What happens next is every bit as low as life got for me.

Yeah, my story sure isn't getting any easier to tell. What happened that night is not my next Intermonial. It wasn't a divine intervention. It was a police intervention. It was an overdue intervention as my life was spiraling out of control.

Feel free to dislike me over what I'm about to tell you (I know I've done my stretch of self-loathing over it), but please respect my honesty. As I said, every word in the book is true. As I am being honest about my personal failings, know that I am also being honest about my Intermonials. That bird incident happened just like I said. So did that steering wheel spinning out of my hands.

On this night I was drinking, sure (Nothing new there), but I remember everything. No blissful fog on this one. Here is what brought me to the worst point of my life. Well, the worst point in my life so far. I still had a ways to go before I hit bottom. That will be my next Intermonial. Before I get there though, I need to spend a couple of weeks in jail- and lose almost everything I care about in this world.

# <u>RING</u>

I saw it was home on the caller ID so I answered my cell, hoping it wasn't an emergency. I sure didn't need any more grief.

It was Ryan. He wanted to go over to his friend Joey's house. Side note: He and Joey were born two days apart and have been friends since they were babies. Ryan wanted to know if Joey's dad could come pick him up and take him over to their house. "It's Friday night Dad! Just for a few hours, please?"

Hmmm? The boy was grounded. I should have told him no. Heck, I should have been home. We should have still been in Michigan. I was wracked with so much well-deserved guilt that I made him a deal. "You can go over to Joey's house until ten o'clock (city curfew). Be home before then. And you can only go if you clean the kitchen table and pick those couch cushions off the living room floor though. I don't want our place messy when Joey's dad walks in. I'll be home soon."

That's not word for word, and we always said, 'I love you' before we hung up, but that was the basic gist of the deal. My focus went back to the nasty chick across the bar that was giving me hard looks. *What was her problem?*

I never did find that out. I had a few more beers, chased skirts when they came around, and talked sports with the guys when the girls didn't. I do remember the nasty woman standing by the door when I left. She was still giving me hard looks and I remember leaving upset. If drunken memory serves, it was around ten o'clock.

I adjusted my dew rag (no helmet-law in Arizona), dawned my sunglasses, got on my Honda, and rode home to talk to Ryan. When I walked in the door, the first thing I saw was the dirty kitchen table. A quick glance at the living room and the couch cushions were still scattered about the floor, only with new dirty clothes added to for effect. You know, to complete the white-trash look.

The apartment was empty. No sign of Ryan. No sign of Jared. I already had enough grief from the management, accusing my poor innocent babies (sarcasm alert) of vandalizing the pool area after hours. Both boys knew they had to be inside by ten o'clock. No later. It was well past that.

I started walking around the complex, asking kids if they'd seen either one of them. Now I was angry with both kids. After an eternity of stressing out (probably about five minutes), Jared showed up. "Hi, dad!"

"Why aren't you home?" It's after ten-o'-freakin' clock! Where's

Ryan?"

And so I went... yelling at my youngest boy. Chris Blizzard, The Bar Fly (who used to be a good dad, I swear), getting more and more furious as I paced around.

It was sometime after ten-thirty when Ryan got home. Joey was still with him, so apparently his night out wasn't finished. It was finished as far as I was concerned though. I pounced on him the moment he walked inside.

"Look at this kitchen! I give you the night off from being grounded and all I ask is that you clean this s**t up before Joey's dad gets here. And this is what you give me?" Again, this isn't word for word. I'm trying to keep the book at least PG-13. But I was in his face and shaking with rage.

I expected apologies. I demanded apologies. It didn't matter what lame excuse he gave me this time. Joey was going home and Ryan was going to clean up this mess and go to bed. I'd had enough!

For the life of me, I can't remember what he said. I know it went through my head over and over the next two weeks as I paced my cellblock, but that memory has since escaped my brain. It was something along the lines, "What's your problem?" Actually, that may be an exact quote after all. Either way, it's close enough. It sent me over the edge.


# [PAUSE]


The moment is here. Not my next Intermonial, the moment I tore my life down the rest of the way. The family I made, with help from Fatneck of course, but the Blizzard boys were a family because of me. I built us. Now, in true Chris Blizzard fashion, I was tearing us down. Oh, we would be a family again after what happens next. Ryan and I are very close today. But as for what happens next… again, know that if I can bear such a moment of shame, when I tell you about the steering wheel or the bird, I'm being just as honest. And I promise to make sense out of all this by the time we're done. Okay, that may be a little much. But I'll try to make sense of it. That feels more accurate. Now, back to my regularly scheduled demise. Already in progress...

# [RESUME]

"What's my problem?" (Good question, actually) That was not the groveling I expected from him. Instead, he stared at me, unflinching, unafraid.

I was afraid though. His disregarding chores and rules had been hard enough, but now he was in my face. He was nearly as big as me and looked ready to fight. In my drunken head, he was challenging me. It was a showdown.

I threw my beer towards his face. Distracted by that, I sucker-punched him with a right cross. Yes, I sucker-punched my own kid. It sent him down and scrambling back out the door. I chased after him and Joey, telling neither one of them to come back. They didn't, but the cops did.

It was about twenty minutes later when they knocked. I opened the door, beer in hand, Jared standing next to me. Long story short, they took me to jail, and Jared to Bula's.

# Chapter 19 Lockdown

## Judge Angry

My first stop at *Arrest Night* was the Scottsdale Jail. When I was being booked, an officer asked me for my version of what happened. I asked him if there was anything I could tell him that would convince him to take me home and forget all about this. He laughed and said, "No." I told him in that case I had nothing to say. He took pictures and prints and then locked me up for the night.

The next day I found myself in front of a very angry judge. She looked at the paperwork in front of her and sighed loud enough I thought it should have been added to the transcripts. After getting decidedly ticked off, she looked at me hard and said, "We have a special section for child abusers. The bond is set at $100,000. Next."

That was it. I don't even remember if she even asked me if I was guilty or not. To me, that price seemed kind of high for hitting my kid. Sure I was guilty, but calling me a child abuser seemed awfully judgmental- even for a judge. After all, this was my initial arraignment.

What I didn't know was the extent of the criminal record she was looking at. Apparently, a very bad man had been arrested and used my social security number. That left me showing five previous felonies, one of which was 'methamphetamine manufacture with children present'. I was dismissed and taken to another cell. This one was in cellblock four, a special section for child abusers to keep them safe from the general population.

The next day, Child Protective Services asked me to sign over custody of my kids to their grandpa Jasper. How could I argue about my parental rights when I was wearing pink underwear and a pink jailhouse jumpsuit? It's not like their grandpa wanted any of this. He was stepping up because his grandkids needed him. I was in jail. His daughter, Fatneck, was in jail- on an unrelated matter, and again, not relevant to our story. I signed the papers and Jasper brought them back to live with him and his wife in Draginaw, Michigan.

# I Thought I Thought

In jail, my daily routine went something like this; I woke up and started pacing in my cell. At some point, they opened our doors and I paced the corridor of Cell Block 4. Then I ate breakfast, which was the most tasteless meal imaginable. No salt. No pepper. They didn't even add sugar to the powdered drink. Then it was back to pacing. Because of the layout of bolted-down tables, I couldn't pace in any sort of circle pattern, which is my preferred pacing route. It was thirty-seven steps straight to one wall; then thirty-seven steps straight back to the other. Then repeat, again and again.

My fellow inmates did two basic activities; they played cards and invented things. It was amazing to see all the things they could do with common, basic items. When I watched a guy make a tortilla out of some old bread, while two other guys offered advice on how to make it better, I knew I was looking at people with too much time on their hands. It was sad how many of them seemed at ease like they belonged there.

Not me. I paced back and forth like someone with someplace else place to be. I walked back and forth in front of the cellblock so much, that a guy told me I would escape by wearing out the concrete. If I had been in there long enough, I probably would have. I just laughed, nodded, and kept pacing and thinking. Well, I thought I was thinking. But I was really just pacing. I am quite sure God was hoping I would do some introspection during this time, but I didn't. Oh, there were plenty of prayer groups in jail and I eagerly jumped in when I could. Sure I was asking for help (weren't we all?), but I wasn't listening. I wasn't doing any soul-searching. I did my time. That's what I did... and I paced.

To break the monotony I would sometimes use the pay phone. Since every call had to be sent collect and cost the person you were dialing approximately one million dollars to connect, I didn't do that very often. When I did, there were basically three different people I called; Bula, 'Ma' (my ex-mother-in-law), Jim, 'Dad' (My ex-father), and Aaron, 'Ray' (The brother I shot with my first BB gun- the Ray gun).

In the end, Bula put her townhouse up as collateral for the bail loan and Jim paid a fee (approximately $1,300 cash) to a bail bondsman. After two hours of out-processing, I was issued my 'personals' back and released into the Arizona sun, free at last free at last... and lit a cigarette. After two weeks of pacing in jail and not thinking I paced on the sidewalk outside the jail, smoking a cigarette... still not thinking. Sure, I blamed myself for the fight with Ryan, but I saw it as a momentary lapse in judgment, not as a symptomatic reflection of how my life was spinning out of control because of my drinking.

# Good Bridges

I had two jobs when I got out of jail. All of them were with employers from my past. I was back to a full-time job with The Printing Shop where I had worked for twelve years, before Attila. I was also working at Roy's, running a press part-time. Yes, the same company I had quit The Printing Shop to work for at the end of the Attila era. It was part-time, good money, and easy work. Actually, it was the best and easiest job I've ever had. I ran a big old Heidelberg printing press... one that liked to be run slowly. I would load paper, flip some levers and it would print for upwards of forty minutes without stopping. Every once in a while I would pull a sheet of paper to *press check*; that left me all kinds of time to do crossword puzzles or clean my golf clubs and shotguns, eat lunch, watch TV, etc. Everything about that place was casual. My friendship with Roy included. Thank God we were friends. I sure needed him that afternoon.

# A Very Long Day

Bula, bless her heart, picked me up from the jail and brought me home to Fancy Schmancyville. It had been a long two weeks and I needed a day of smoking cigarettes, walking around outside, and checking in the refrigerator, if for no other reason than I could. There was a note on my door telling me *Helga*, in the front office, needed to talk to me. The long and short of our talk was this; she knew about my fight with Ryan, subsequent arrest, and stint in jail. She told me I had until the end of the day to be completely moved out. Apparently, violent alcoholics/convicts aren't welcome in Fancyland. Go figure.

I called Roy and God bless him, he brought over his truck, trailer, and moving buddy. I rented a storage unit for my household belongings and by that evening everything was moved out of my apartment and I was back living with Bula.

# Kids Better Off

A few days later I had my own apartment. The boys were in Michigan, enrolled in a school that was nearly identical to Hemlock. They were living with their retired grandfather who was in his mid-sixties and had spent his life working as a plumber. He was married to his second wife who was much younger than him and worked full-time in a job that demanded a lot of travel and time away from home. It may not have been the 'ideal' situation, but it was a lot better than life with a drunken, angry dad who was more focused on paying his bar tab than raising his children.

I was living in a one-bedroom apartment with Moxie while working at the first print shop I had ever worked at, back when I had that fight with Harry Winters. They still wouldn't let me near the delivery truck, but they let me run their printing presses. I may have lost the battle with Greg over my job there back in 1986, but he was long gone. Bob, the owner, was still there though and he and I were still solid. I don't know if he knew I had just gotten out of jail or not, but even if he did, Bob still would have hired me back. Since my brother and I had worked for him before, he knew that despite whatever personal issues we might have going on; Blizzards are good workers.

Then I got offered my dream job. Remember Roy's print shop I went to work at right before Attila and I split? I worked for them part-time over the years and was working there part-time when the kids and I came back from Michigan. In a secret dinner meeting one night the owner of the shop, *Thurman*, told a co-worker and me about his idea. Basically, he was very unhappy with the way Roy was running the printing side of his business. He and his son were delighted every time I came in to work because they knew things would get done right and on time. His plan was to fire Roy and Roy's brother and father as well as the typesetter. The next day, I would be put in charge of Roy's job and the other guy would be the new typesetter. I knew I could do the job in less than thirty hours/week so I had Thurman promise to pay me a minimum forty-hour check, as well as overtime pay when I worked past forty hours. That way I had a guaranteed minimum eight hundred dollar paycheck every Friday

# A Visit From Father Jim

Sometime between my release from jail and the date of my next Intermonial (December 23, 2005), Jim Crab (still 'dad' at the time) came out from Texas to visit me in Arizona for a couple of days. He stayed at a hotel and we barhopped together. I thought it was a good time. Looking back I can see that he was there to assess my life. Back then, I was too far gone to notice that I was being evaluated. I simply saw him as an old drinking buddy who came to reminisce. Drink and reminisce. And that's what we did.

# Chapter 20 Bailing Out Blizzard

## (Intermonial #4)

I thought I had lost everything when Fancyland evicted me, fresh out of jail and childless. Then came December 23, 2005. It was two days before Christmas and three days before my thirty-ninth birthday. I don't remember much about that day so I have to go by medical records and what people told me, but I can tell you this much for certain, God bailed me out again.

The only memory I have of that day was eating lunch at work. It was a Friday and the boss had lunch catered by a Mexican restaurant. I remember the food was delicious. I had a couple of shots of really old booze that Bob had bought for his son. That's about it. The rest of the day is blank.

Here's what I assume about that day... I got up and went to work on my motorcycle (my car wouldn't pass emissions and the plates were expired). I ran the press all day, had that lunch I told you about, and knowing me, I went home. Still knowing me, I drank beer. I showered, put on my leather jacket, motorcycle boots, and fingerless riding gloves, then dawned on my dew rag and wrap-around sunglasses, got back on my motorcycle, and headed for the bar.

Here's what I can piece together through medical reports, what I was told, and logical speculation. After work, I went to The *Woodchipper*- a bar I was frequenting at the time. I'm sure I had a few more beers at the bar, but probably not hard liquor. Then around 10:30, a "random" ambulance found me lying on the side of the road, next to my downed motorcycle. I was at the Price Road and the 202 intersections. I should have been at Priest and the 202, but I must have gotten confused.

Anyway, here's what happened, again, according to what I was told:

An ambulance driver and another EMT (Emergency Medical Technician- my new heroes) saw my overturned motorcycle on the road. "This doesn't look right," The driver said, turned on the Whirly lights and stopped. They found me lying off to the side of the road, not breathing.

From there to the emergency room at Scottsdale Healthcare, even with a V-8 engine and flashy lights, it must have taken the better part of fifteen minutes to get me to the hospital. During the ride, one EMT kept pumping fresh air into my lungs (God bless him) but I wasn't breathing again until the ER resuscitated me. Obviously, my heart kept beating through all of this, otherwise, my brain would have gone bad. I don't know how long a person can last without breathing, but that ambulance must have happened right after my crash. That or God kept me fresh.

Either way, I believe God sent that ambulance. He might have even sent me down Price Road instead of Priest. But if I had taken the right road, maybe I wouldn't have crashed. Perhaps, but maybe I was supposed to crash. I sure didn't learn anything from the two weeks I spent in jail, losing my kids and getting evicted from my apartment. Talk about ignoring the bird. I couldn't ignore this bird though. This bird locked its talons into me, scooped me off that bike, and dropped me on my un-helmeted head... hard!

Metaphors aside, what actually happened is anyone's guess. According to medical records, my BAC (Blood Alcohol Content) was .14. Sure, that's drunk- nearly twice the legal limit- but I was an everyday drinker and longtime biker. At that level, I didn't just lose my balance and fall over. Someone probably hit me with a car. It wouldn't surprise me if they were drinking too. No one called it in. I bet the drunk simply apologized for driving with their lights off, turned them on, wished me the best of luck, and drove away.

When I crashed my Mustang at Fort Campbell- when God ripped the steering wheel out of my hands, also in the car were two screaming and terrified passengers who didn't deserve to die. God saved all three of us that night, but which one of us was He saving? That question has nagged me ever since my crash at Ft. Campbell in 1987. The night the 'random' ambulance showed up, I was alone. Since I don't remember anything, I obviously wasn't feeling any pain when I was lying there. God could have just let me slip away. Instead, He sent trained EMTs with a van full of life-saving equipment. God saved me.

# Intermonial in Review:

This one a skeptic could easily dismiss as pure luck. As you will read later, two clergymen do. But just like I know that interrupting a phone call was the work of God, I also know that the ambulance showing up was God as well. Why would God save me, especially after all the sinning I've done? Keep reading. I will get to that. I honestly believe I've figured out why He has always been there for me. And again, you can decide for yourself whether I'm right- after you've heard my story.

# Chapter 21 While you were sleeping

Following my crash night, I spent the next two weeks in a coma. The hospital tracked down my family in Michigan and told them what they knew: *Chris Blizzard was found on the side of the road, not breathing*. They didn't know how long I wasn't breathing or how much (if any) brain damage I had. There was no way of knowing whether I would wake from my coma or if I would ever get out of bed again. It was simply too early to tell.

In step the Blizzards. God bless 'em, everyone. Old *dish-it-out-and-take-it* Matt Blizzard was right there to take care of his little brother, again. Aaron, two years older than Matt, and four years older than me, was also right there to help out little bro. As was my little sister, Sharon.

Matt came out from Michigan to put my life on hold. He explained what happened to the front office at Sunquench, broke my lease, and moved all of my belongings into a storage unit. He, Aaron, and my dad all pitched in the money to pay off my cell phone bill and break my contract early. Then they hunkered down to wait.

Aaron, who lived in Maryland, and Matt, who lived in Michigan, both took a leave of absence from work and stayed out in Arizona to watch my progress. I don't know how much I 'progressed' during my coma, but from what everyone tells me, I sure did talk a lot.

I guess I was pretty still the first week. Then I woke up enough to pull out my hoses and needles. That's when nurses restrained my hands and feet and put me in a drug-induced coma. Whatever drugs they were giving me to keep me asleep, apparently removed the breaks from my mouth too. Suddenly I instantly relayed any thoughts (and I mean any) that passed through my brain. That's when the babbling started. From sexual propositions to my nurses to claiming I was a military pilot who needed to be untied so I could fly my mission, most of the things that left my mouth were pretty crazy. For the record... I blame the drugs. I also deeply apologize to all of the staff in the ICU at Scottsdale Healthcare. Thanks for not pulling the plug. You all have the patience of saints... even when you have patients from hell.

I would also like to thank Sharon for coming out from Michigan to see me during my coma. I told her that I didn't remember the visit. She said, "That's too bad bro. We had some deep conversations during your coma." Makes me wonder what I said.

Well, that's what the Blizzards were up to; gathering around me. My extended family, however, was another matter. What I'm about to tell you is a mixture of fact and speculation. I promised you in the beginning that every word in this book is true. And it is! So is my speculation.

Whether I'm right or wrong is a matter of opinion. From here on this story is going to change gears a little. Until now I have been sharing with you things I experienced first-hand. I will continue to do that, but many of the things that are about to happen to me I will never fully understand. All I can do is try to relate actions to motives; what I experienced to why. I will do my level best to stay clear on what is fact and what is my interpretation.

Here's a fact; Grandpa Jasper had a fight with Jared over Christmas. I don't know all the details of what happened, but apparently, Jared thought he got gipped on presents and threw a fit. In Jasper's defense, that sounds like a 'Jared' thing to do. I can see how it could have sent

Grandpa over the edge. Jared's ungrateful attitude could press anyone's buttons.

After his tantrum, Jasper flew Jared down to Florida to live with Clog Crab (now, Clog Cockroach) during the first few days of my coma. Jasper was a retired man in his sixties. His wife was in her thirties and worked in Southern Michigan, often spending the entire week away from home. God bless him, Jasper mostly wanted to sit around and drink beer. He worked hard his whole life and he deserved the rest. He wasn't prepared to be a full-time dad. He should never have been put in that position to begin with. He stepped up when I was in jail. He drove out to Arizona, picked up the two boys, and brought them back to live with him and his wife in Michigan; a very decent act. No doubt about it.

As for his ex-wife Bula (ma), she had Moxie... and a big surprise waiting for me. I'll get to that as soon as I get out of this coma.

As for Jim Crab- my former foster father and dad for a time, I have to speculate as to what he and his brood did during my coma. I know they thought about me. I don't know if they prayed. That would be some grand speculation there, but I know they came up with plans for my children and me. They come up with some real humdingers, actually. I believe they mostly sprang from Jim Crab though. He came up with those on his own. He decided what needed to be done and convinced the rest to go along with him. Yes, I'm in speculation mode, but I'll bet I'm also right. You be the judge.

# Chapter 22 Recovery Ward 101

Okay, time to wake up. I swear everything in my life is a story. You wouldn't believe how many I've skipped so far. Even the way I came out of my coma is another typical Chris Blizzard scene. This one I want to relive though... if nothing else, just to see Svetlana again.

We all know how people are supposed to come out of a coma... it's in plenty of movies. They wake up, surrounded by friends and family, and immediately remember the last thing that happened before the bus ran them down. *Did I save the child?* is the first thing old Charlie wants to know.

Not me, man. My first conscious memory was sitting up in bed with Svetlana, just gabbing away. I have no idea what I was talking about. All I know is I had a cute Russian girl sitting in bed with me. Her friend was sitting in a chair across the room. To this day I have no idea how I convinced her to get in bed with me. I also don't know what I was saying when I woke up, but I sure had their attention. They were both cute and I was happy. The first thing I remember saying... my first conscious words if you will, were, "Excuse me. I gotta pee." I tossed back the covers, got out of bed, stood up, took a step, and fell on my face. I couldn't walk.

"Oh no, let us help you." the girls said, rushing to my aide.

"I'd appreciate that," I said, not wondering why I couldn't walk, just needing to pee... and grateful for any help I could get.

They helped me to my feet, and with a girl under each arm, I was able to shuffle and hobble to the urinal. The girls looked away while I did my business, but held on to me so I wouldn't fall... God bless 'em.

When I finished, they got me back to bed and I went straight to sleep. No questions asked.

Don't ask me how I know (I must have spotted a clock) but that was about three in the morning. When I woke up again around seven-thirty, one of the nurses brought me a wheelchair and helped me into it. Again, I didn't ask any questions. I was just grateful to be mobile. I remembered falling earlier so I knew my legs didn't work. It stood to reason I needed a wheelchair. And someone helping me with it was much appreciated.

It rolled nice too. My bed was in an open ward so I had lots of room to play with my new toy. One good push would send me a long way. I swerved around nurses and patients until I got to a clear path. Then I would go for speed.

I never thought about where I was. I didn't wonder why I was in a hospital. I didn't wonder why I couldn't walk. I just wheeled myself around and said hello to anyone and everyone. "Look at my chair! Isn't that cool? How are you? Nice to meet you. I'm fine, thanks. Have you seen Svetlana?"

Mr. Ball, meet Mrs. Peen

I had just been assigned a room when Bula walked in. "Hi, ma! How do you like my chair?"

"Do you know why you're in a wheelchair?" she asked.

"Because I can't walk."

"Do you know why you can't walk?"

"Because... because I fall down when I try?" *Hmmm, that was a good question.*

"Do you even know where you are?"

*That was another good question.* "It looks like a hospital."

"It is. Do you know why you're in a hospital?"

"No. Do you?"

"Yes. You were in a motorcycle accident. You've been in a coma."

"Really? How long?"

"Two weeks."

"Is my bike here?"

"No, you're motorcycle was impounded from the crash scene."

"That's just great. Now, how am I going to get to work?"

Side note: The conversation moved about this quickly. Of course, this is done from the memory of a drug-laden brain, but my recollection of our talk is pretty close... exact in some spots. She really did lay it on me that hard and fast.

"You don't have a job."

"Then I need to go home."

"You don't have a home anymore, either. Matt moved all your stuff into storage and broke your lease. I have your dog. Jasper has Ryan. Clog has Jared. Do you even remember your kids? You lost everything. You're lucky you didn't get arrested again. You were drunk. Your driver's license is automatically suspended for two years because you were in a coma. That's state law. Count your blessings all you have is brain damage. I'm already late for work. I'll stop in to see you later. Love ya! Bye."

Dang.

Suddenly my chair looked different. I won't pretend to remember what I was thinking, but I know my head was swirling when she left. The room phone rang. Hmm? That must be my phone. I wheeled over and scooped it off the receiver. "Hello?"

"Hey, bro! How are ya?" Matt asked.

"I'm doing great! I got a wheelchair. I can't walk. Bula was just he—"

"Do you even know who this is?" he interrupted.

"I have no idea, but I'd sure like to."

"This is your brother Matt. What do you mean Bula was there?"

"Yeah, she just left. She told me all about the crash and how you moved all my stuff out of my apartment for me. Thanks, bro."

"That expletive!" he yelled. "I told her not to tell you what happened! I was going to do that."

"Oh, it's cool bro. She just told me what happened. Hey, I needed to know sometime, right? It sure explains why I can't walk and why I have such a cool wheelchair. I'd like to ride this baby down some hills."

It wasn't cool with Matt though. He had given her specific instructions not to tell me what had happened if she stopped by the hospital when I woke up. He knew it would be a shock to me- to say the least- and he wanted to break it to me slowly. He cursed a few more minutes, said goodbye, and came straight to the hospital from his motel. Aaron came with him and we had a brother's reunion. They were glad to see me alive and I was just happy to see my bros. I still couldn't grasp what happened. That would sink in over the next two months- in the recovery ward.

After hours of visiting and catching up on old times, Aaron gave me a cell phone with his and Matt's numbers programmed in. They were both staying in town and told me to call if I needed anything. Otherwise, they would be back to see me tomorrow. Before they left, they helped me to the urinal for one last wobbly pee jaunt.

Nurse *Dino* came in right behind them to introduce himself and let me know that anytime I needed help (you know, like getting to the bathroom) to just push "That little yeller button right next to ya over there." Oh no.

I didn't know this yet, but a few things changed in me since my crash. Mind you, this was still day one of coming out of my coma. I had no idea that bumping my head could make my prostrate enlarge, but ever since my crash I pee a lot. As a matter of fact, I pee all the time. TMI? Sorry. Anyway, here I was sitting up with my hospital bed inclined, watching TV. *Hmmm, I had to pee again already?*

No problem. The call button is *right there over there*. Old Dino is a big boy. Not too bright, maybe, but I didn't need Albert Einstein to go pee. I didn't even need two cute cleaning ladies under each arm to get to the restroom. I guessed old Dino could keep me from falling over all by himself. Push button. Wait.

Wait. Watch more TV. Wait. Push more buttons. Wait. Push all the buttons. That got Dino's attention.

After I explained to a flustered Dino why I had to push the "Help-me-I'm-dying" button, he finally calmed down and helped me to the bathroom. My two cute cleaning ladies turned away when I did my business. Not Dino. No, he had to look at what I was fidgeting for.

Embarrassing, as it is to reveal, I had a bit of slippage right before I hit the panic button. When Dino saw the little yellow spot on the front of my underwear, he said "Looks like someone had a little accident."

*Looks like someone had a little accident.* That comment stays with me. It's a classic. I didn't know what to do or say. I had my right arm around this guy, needing him to hold me up. Trying to grab the back of his skull and slamming his face into the wall would have been pointless. All I would have done was go into a backspin. I would have crashed on the floor and embarrassed myself. Or I could have gotten in his face, figuratively and literally, about how my little accident was his fault.

I could have done either one of those things, but I did neither. Instead, I let him help me back to bed, thanked him, and listened to him lecture me on which buttons I should never push. Then he left, leaving my door open, as is standard.

If this story were fiction I would now tell you about a wonderful moment of realization I had, having lost everything, nearly my own life included. I would tell you about my moment of clarity when the past, present, and future all became clear. And from that inspiring moment, I marched forward.

But this is my life. Until lately, I've never been much of a reflective sort. I sure wasn't one then. What I was though, and what I have always been; is a fighter. I'd been down before. Okay maybe not this low, but I knew hard times. I never did have sense enough to quit. This time was no exception. It was just another setback.

The bathroom issue was the first thing I needed to address. I swung my legs out of bed and stood up. Holding onto the side rails for support, I hobbled and bobbled (shuffling my feet) along it. Once around the U of the footboard and back to the wall on the other side of the headboard, I would reverse course and do it again. The more I did it, the easier it got. Then a nurse spotted me.

"Why are you out of bed? What are you doing? Get back in bed or your wheelchair! You could hurt yourself!" Etc. Within minutes, about half a dozen more nurses were standing at my door, yelling at me. They pointed out all the sharp corners I could hit my head on if I fell.

"Then give me a room where I can I can do this without all the sharp edges. I will gladly go and learn how to walk there," I offered.

"There is no one available right now to take you to the physical therapy room, Mr. Blizzard. You are scheduled to be in there tomorrow. Someone will be there with you to make sure you don't hurt yourself. Please get back in bed or your wheelchair."

"Are you going to take me to go pee any time I need to?" Before anyone could answer I continued... "Are any of you going to follow me around the rest of my life making sure I don't fall down? Making sure I can go pee before I piss myself? Which one you are going home with me when I get released?" This time I waited for an answer. When no one did, I said, "That's what I thought. I've fallen down before. I'll fall down again. If I do it here, I'll try to do it gracefully. When you can take me to the rehab room, I'll go. Until then I'm just going to keep teaching myself how to walk again. And unless you're going to tie me back down or drug me, you can't stop me."

I continued shuffling around the bed and they continued yelling at me. After a couple of minutes, they finally lost their steam and went back to the nurse's station, which happened to be located right outside my door. That made it difficult for them to ignore my self-prescribed physical therapy, but God bless 'em, they found a way to pretend there wasn't a potential lawsuit hobbling around the bed in room 421. They went back to work and I kept putting one foot in front of the other. It's what I do.

The next day (or thereabouts... memory is a little foggy here) Aaron and Matt were back. Impressed as we all were with my bed hobbling, I still needed the wheelchair to be mobile. I got into it myself and asked Aaron to push me.

The three of us spent hours going up and down the streets of Old Town Scottsdale, visiting shops, and eating out. Side note: According to the hospital I wasn't supposed to smoke, even off grounds. I have been a smoker since I was seven years old. I'm a smoker now. For the two months I spent in recovery though, I didn't smoke. Not so much as a puff. I promised the nurses I wouldn't... and I kept my word.

I would like to give a great big thank you to all the nurses on the fourth-floor recovery ward at Scottsdale Healthcare. Oh, and the people in the ER who brought me back. I would also like to send another thanks to the people in the ICU for taking such good care of my foul mouth and me during my coma. Thanks to everyone at Scottsdale Healthcare. You're the best! Well, except Dino. You suck.

Back to the story... by day three or four I was walking again. The hallway went in a rectangle that made a circumference around a host of rooms. Once I was able to complete an entire lap, holding on to the wall for balance, I never sat in that ugly wheelchair again. It wasn't cute anymore.

# The circle of life

My daily life in recovery was pretty much like my life in jail. I woke up and paced. When a meal was ready, I ate. Then I went back to pacing my rectangular track. I knew every person in every room. Well, at least I knew the basics of them. Some you couldn't talk to. Everyone knew me though. I was the *Walking Man*. When I saw someone in a wheelchair, I always offered to push. Some people let me push them during my laps. Eventually, they would get bored and I'd drop them back in their room. We would shake hands or hug and I'd go back to walking. For variety, I would sometimes reverse direction and do my laps clockwise.

After Aaron went back to Maryland and Matt to Michigan, my main visitor was Bula (Then 'ma'). One day she even brought Moxie! God bless her. And God bless the people at the hospital who let him in. I got to see my old friend.

Clog flew in from Florida. I can't remember if she brought her husband, Satchel, but she didn't bring my son, Jared. For some reason that didn't work into their plans. The last I heard, Satchel Cockroach was making upwards of $1,000,000/year between salary and bonuses, so it wasn't a money issue that kept them from bringing him. For reasons that are unclear to this day, they didn't bring him to see his dad- who he hadn't seen since the night I got in a fight with Ryan. Nope, them not bringing Jared should have been a warning that something was wrong, but I was full of love and trust; not to mention how distracted I was fighting my own battles at the time.

She had taken in my youngest son during my coma... the son I had lost because I got drunk and punched his brother. No, I didn't begrudge her in the least for not bringing Jared. She was coming to help me... just like the Blizzards had come to my side. That's what family does when you need them. Oh, she wasn't a "real" family, but she used to be my foster sister. She was there for me now. She was there for my kid. What's not to love and trust?

Jim Crab came out to see me too. He already helped bail me out of jail. His daughter had my kid. Now, when the hospital released me, he wanted to bring me to Texas so I could start my life over with him and Lulu. Wow, everyone was coming to my side.

Jim, the ever-vigilant moneyman, even did my taxes while I was in the hospital. Sure it was only February and taxes didn't need to be done until April 15, but Jim was so concerned with helping me out that he got them filed with three months to spare. I even had about five thousand bucks worth of refund coming. Can you feel the love?

# Chapter 23 Alone Star

That's basically how things stood when I got discharged from the hospital around the end of February 2006. Jim suggested I sell off the things I had in storage (a life's worth of furniture and memories) so I wouldn't have a hundred-dollar monthly storage bill. However, he took one look inside the overstuffed storage unit Matt had packed my belongings into and quickly banished the thought of having a giant moving sale before we left. He was so committed to bringing me to Texas though; he didn't even seem interested in building me an exit strategy from his home. That's commitment. That's love. So I thought.

Pave the road with intervention

William Shakespeare once said, "The road to hell is paved with good intentions." That's true, Bill, but it's also paved with bad intentions. I didn't know then and I don't know now, exactly what Father Jim Crab's intentions were for me when I came out of my coma. He certainly had a road paved for me though. That's why I say he did a lot of thinking during my coma, but I don't believe he did much praying. I don't believe the God I know and love told him to take me to Texas and pull my life out from underneath me. I'm also sure He didn't tell Jim to rip my family apart. No, other than perhaps the devil whispering in his ear, Jim Crab came up with that intervention idea all on his own.

Welcome back to *Fogland*. This is where things get hazy again. Not drunk hazy, but foggy so I couldn't see what was going on around me. I will tell the facts straight and give you my interpretations of them as I go. As with my Intermonials, you are invited to agree or disagree with my conclusions. I only promise honesty. And a few more Intermonials.

I would also like to remind you that I'm not very bright. Not only did

I trust and love these people, but also - as a guy who dug a foxhole in a latrine, I'm simply not very smart. As I take you through my time in Texas, I'm sure you would do things differently. At times you might wonder when I'll quit being so dumb. In my defense, I'm full of love, trust, and stupidity. That, my friend, is a combination of characteristics that's bound for trouble.

# Texas Dreamin'

Thurman sent his boy to visit me in the hospital. His son told me they would postpone firing Roy and his clan until I got my health back. Then we would go ahead with the plan we hashed out that night over dinner. It wasn't just about getting rid of Roy... they wanted me! I say again, Blizzards are good workers. If you get a chance to hire one, do it.

Yeah, in Phoenix, I was leaving behind the best job I had ever had, but there were other printing jobs in Texas. I put that in the past and looked forward to starting life over in another state; surrounded by people who loved me. I've never remarried and I wasn't involved with anyone when I crashed. My kids were spread around the country and I didn't have a home. Other than my dream job, I had nothing to hold me to Phoenix. Should I go for the dream job and perhaps fall back into my bad ways, or surround myself with family and love while starting over in the awesome state of Texas? That's what I weighed. Texas won out. From the hospital, it seemed like the best choice. Actually, it felt like the only choice.

# Intervention?

It wasn't an intervention. That gives Jim Crab implied credit for trying to help me. After all, that is the purpose of an intervention right, to help someone. Where are the good intentions my road to hell was supposedly paved with? I've had years to think about my time in Texas and to this day I don't see how any benefits were ever intended for me. And I sure didn't feel the love either. I didn't feel that from the moment I walked into their igloo.

It was a cold house, literally. Jim loved his air conditioning. The house was cold when I went to bed. When I woke up it was cold. It was cold all day long. It wasn't as cold as his truck though. Riding in the front seat with *snowzilla* blowing on me (Air conditioning always on max, regardless of outside temperature) required thermal gear. Whenever he said we were going for a ride, I put on my winter coat and zipped it up. I told him I was freezing, but that didn't even take me from a four to a three on the fan speed. Closing the vents on my side of the cab saved me a direct blow, but I still froze. Every time.

It was cold in that house figuratively too. Lulu greeted me with a brief hug and said it was nice to see me. She used to be full of love and warmth. She was the opposite of Jim. When he said 'no,' she said, 'yes.' Buford and I learned not to ask Jim for anything... unless she made us. *If you have to ask, ask Lulu*. That was our philosophy. He was hard. She was soft. Nowadays, he's still hard and she's well; I don't really know her anymore. I can't say who or what she is. To me she stands as proof of the old adage, *if you dance with the devil long enough, the devil doesn't change, the devil changes you*. In other words, I think she's danced with Jim too long.

When she greeted me and said nice to see you, I expected her to follow that up with questions like, "How are you? How are you feeling after your accident? How was the trip?" I was all set to tell her that I was fine and thank her for taking me in. But she didn't ask me how I was doing. As a matter of fact, no one did. From the time I came out of my coma right up until today, not one soul in that entire family has ever asked me how I was doing. Not once. If you pass a person on the street, you might nod your head and say, "How ya doin'?" But if someone you love comes out of a coma... you certainly ask, "How are you doing?" They didn't ask me though. They didn't ask me anything. They only told me how I was doing. And I was always doing terrible.

# Hope for Tomorrow

Mind you, I went there full of hope. I was excited to start my life over and get things right this time. Alcohol was the furthest thing from my mind. It's like the drinking bug got knocked right out of my un-helmeted head when I crashed. The docs told me I was lucky the road punched a hole in the center of my forehead. It acted as a pressure relief valve to give my swelling brain a place to go. I think my drinking bug got pushed out too, because I haven't been drunk since.

I figured I would hang around with the *folks* until I got the five thousand dollars I had coming from my tax return. Then I would buy a car and find a job. After a couple of months of living rent-free, I would have enough money saved to get an apartment and send for my kids.

I thought I had a good plan. Hooray, I was going to be a Texan! A sober Texan who takes care of his kids... just like I used to. No more ruining my life over booze. No more running away. That was the old me. That was the drunk me. That died the night I crashed. I knew that

177

in the hospital.

# Brainwashing Basics

What I didn't know in the hospitals, is what Father Jim's indentations for me were. I still don't. It sure wasn't to help me rebuild my life. Well, unless he was going to let me rebuild it after he tore it down. Again, that's giving his *good* intentions the benefit of the doubt.

I don't know much about brainwashing, but from what I understand, the first thing to do is separate the subject from everything and everyone they know. Once that's done, you tear them down. It stands to reason that in order to build a "new" person, you must first destroy the "old" person. Let me share a typical conversation with Jim and you can decide his intentions for yourself.

Since we are both smokers, most of our talks took place on his patio. To this day I believe that during those talks, Father Jim was sitting on the devil's knee, and I was sitting in God's lap. God had his big old arms around me, protecting me from someone with bad intentions that I loved and trusted completely.

# Unwinnable

During my first few days in *Auschwitz*, Texas, I played a game of Scrabble with Lulu and her mom, Penelope. According to Jim, Penelope was a world-class scrabble player and there would be no shame in losing to her. "Don't get discouraged. Just have fun," he told me.

This was my first time playing Scrabble and since I was obviously brain-damaged, I needed to keep my expectations low. Well, I beat them both... quite handily really. Certainly, that would be counted as evidence of me NOT having brain damage, right? Wrong. "Good game," was the only thing they said. Topic closed. Not, "Oh that's great! Maybe you're not too bad off? Let's see how you do driving?" I didn't need accolades. I knew I was all right. Soon enough, they would be able to tell that too. I thought.

Jim's argument against me getting a job and eventually getting my kids back was simply unwinnable. In the interest of keeping the story moving, let me condense every one of our conversations into one or two. Take this talk and multiply it by one hundred and you have my life in Texas. Well, maybe not that many... after the first month I learned not to bring up getting my life back together. It was a pointless, winless argument. Jim designed it to be winless when I was still in my coma. Our 'conversations' went something like this:

"Can I get a copy of the newspaper so I can start my job search, Dad?"

"Are you kidding? You're in no shape to get a job. You shouldn't even be left unsupervised. You can't go back to work."

"Well, I need to get a job so I can get my kids back."

"Chris, I talked to your doctor. He said there is a sixty percent chance you will never have your life back the way it was. You will always need someone to take care of you."

"Sixty percent?" I asked. "That tells me two things," I deduced. "One, he doesn't know my future. Two, I got a forty percent chance of getting things back to how they were. Can't we focus on the positive side of that one person's opinion?"

"I focus on reality. Not fantasy. You got brain damage. The doctors won't know how extensive it is until after your next CAT scan. And that can't be done until eighteen to twenty-four months from the time of your accident. That way they can compare the new scan to the old scan to determine how much progress you've made."

"So I have to wait eighteen months to two years before they can figure out if I'm okay to go back to work?"

"And get your kids back, yes. I just want to make sure you're ready. Don't rush your recovery. Settle down. Everything is being taken care of for you."

"I know I'm ready to go back to work. Why can't I go now to prove I can do it?"

"Look at your left hand. You can barely use it! You're not ready to work."

Side note: My left hand was weak. True, I didn't have much use for it, but here is my argument against that:

"About five years ago I hurt my left hand (Yes, the same hand) at work when it got infected from a nasty cut. My boss sent me to the same hospital I was in after my accident. The same floor (Recovery Ward) as a matter of fact. I was there for three or four days before they released me. My left hand wasn't much more than a club like it is now, but I made due. I loaded smaller lifts of paper in the press. I was slower than normal, but I got my work done. The more I used my hand, the stronger it got. Within a couple of weeks, it was back to normal. This isn't a similar example of my condition, this is an exact example!"

"There is nothing similar about it," he argued. "You didn't have brain damage then. The doctors will know when you're ready."

"The doctors don't know anything about printing. I've been doing it for nearly twenty years... and I lived through this exact scenario. They can't know what my job entails."

"Oh, they know. You'd be surprised how much they know about doing your job."

"What? They know more about printing than I do?"

"Well, they know as much."

"Teach 'em that in medical school do they?"

"You would be surprised how much they know. Now just relax until we can get another CAT scan done at the VA hospital... in eighteen to twenty-four months."

# Not True

I won't say Jim was lying, but- wait, I will say Jim was lying. He is a lying snake in the grass. There is simply no way a doctor told him that I would have to get another MRI in 18 months to 2 years. I called my brother Aaron and asked him what he knew about MRIs. He told me that my doctor had said to him that unless I was having problems such as headaches, blacking out, etc., they would never do another CAT scan on me. My doctor told Aaron that if I had a tumor growing in my brain it would show up on a scan, but X-rays of my brain couldn't tell them how well my brain was functioning. "The only way they can tell that, Chris, is by giving you cognitive reasoning tests like they did in recovery. Telling you to wait two years for a test that your doctor told me they wouldn't give you is just absurd. How do you do driving?"

"Driving?"

"Doesn't Jim ever take you out in the country and let you drive his truck to see how you do?"

"No," I said, thinking how that was the last thing he would do. If I did good driving his truck, I might be even more determined to go back to work. That was obviously not on Jim's *agenda*. "He would never let me drive his truck. I can't even talk about the future without him telling me I don't have one. I know he wouldn't do anything like that."

At the time I still thought my driver's license was automatically suspended since I was in a coma, like Bula had told me in the hospital. I don't know if she lied or not, but there is no such law. My license was still good.

"It sounds to me, bro," Aaron said, "like Jim's bent on keeping you down. Why?"

"He's just worried about me."

"Taking you out to see if you can drive is the first thing I would do if I were him. This whole situation in Texas feels wrong."

"I think you're being a little paranoid, bro. He's just old and overly protective. He's got my best interests at heart."

God help me, I believed every word of that.

Not God

During one of our "talks," I told Jim what the doctor had told Aaron about me waiting on an MRI they would never do. Jim's reaction, he shook his head and mumbled, "F*****n' Aaron," and walked back inside the house.

"If God sent an ambulance to save me, maybe He also made sure I didn't get brain damage?" I told Jim one day. I thought my argument was sound. During the services in church, Father Jim told his flock (on average about six or eight people, any given Sunday) that I was still alive by the grace of God. His response to my argument about God keeping me from getting brain damage, however, was one that will stay with me forever. This is what he said, word for word.

"God had nothing to do with that ambulance coming along. You just got f****n lucky."

Yes, that is an exact quote. That one sticks with me. If someone else said it, I might not even remember. But to have a priest say that, especially one I loved and respected since high school- was devastating. While I was still grappling with what he said, he went on...

"If you flip a coin twenty-seven times and it turns up heads every time, on the twenty-eighth flip you still have a fifty/fifty chance of flipping tails." ← another exact quote.

Huh? Maybe I *was* brain-damaged because I still didn't understand. I understood the mathematical premise; I just didn't get how it explained why God wasn't there for me the night the ambulance showed up.

I even told him about the bird and what happened the day I ran away from his home back in 1985. I thought maybe he would see that God really was watching out for me. He went on to say he didn't know what happened to Blanca after I left. "One day, she just ran off," he said- ignoring my tale and apparently working through his guilt over getting rid of my dog to punish me for running away.

I was confused now, more than ever. God had nothing to do with that ambulance coming along? *You just got f\*\*\*\*n lucky. I don't know what happened to Blanca. One day she just ran off.*

Hmmm, like me?

"Look kid, you sound confused. If you want to know what you should do, you need to turn to the church clergy for guidance. They have a very close bond with God and are more in tune with what He wants for you."

Huh?

The only clergyman I knew was Jim Crab... and he was telling me God had nothing to do with that ambulance showing up when I was lying on the side of the road not breathing. He was right about one thing; I was confused. I was very confused. I told him I wanted to go back to Arizona.

"If you go back to Arizona, you're f\*\*\*\*d. Don't call us for help because we won't be there. We're there for you now. We won't be if you leave." ← If that isn't an exact quote, it is very close.

As I said, this is a compilation of our many talks/arguments. Some of his points he only made once like his *you just got F\*\*\*\*n lucky* comment. Others were droned into my head over and over. "You got brain damage".

## The Worst of Times

My two months in Auschwitz, TX was far and away the most difficult time of my life. Attila and Basic Training seemed like a field day compared to what Father Jim put me through. I'm talking about a lot more than just the winless arguments too.

Like when Aaron sent me a money order. I asked Jim to take me to my bank so I could put it in my checking account. When we showed up, the teller told me my account had been closed after my AOL monthly deduction left me five dollars overdrawn. The bank closed my account and wouldn't let me reopen it. I went back to his truck, discouraged and dumbfounded. I told Jim the bank closed my account and he said, "Well then, I guess you don't need these." He took a box of blank checks off the seat that the bank had just sent me, walked over to the trashcan, and tossed them away... without so much as shredding them. "I guess I will let you cash it through my account," he said and drove me to his bank, without further discussion.

Side note: After I got back to Arizona I was telling a friend, who used to be a bank manager, about that incident. She told me there was no way a bank would close my account for being overdrawn for less than a week. "The bank wants their money," she explained. "They know they won't get it if they close your account. You would have to be overdrawn for a couple of months before they would do that. Someone else must have closed it. Was anyone else signed on to your account?"

Jim Crab was. Aaron signed him over power of attorney during my hospital stay. Jim had already received one bank statement while I was living with him. I wasn't overdrawn on that one, but it did show my monthly AOL fee being automatically deducted. Jim would have noticed that. I believe (speculation mode again) he waited until the day my account was overdrawn, and then he had it closed. I don't know what he told the bank, but I wasn't allowed to open another account (with any bank) for nearly a year after I left Texas. Whatever he told that bank, it followed me that long. God help me, I really hate that man.

Another violation was when he read my emails. When I first got to his house, I told him my password to my email address when he was helping me log online. He must have put that to memory because, during one of our bouts, he told me that he had been reading my emails. I was primarily writing to one friend and I told her how sad I was living in Texas. As I recall, that was pretty much the content of every email I sent. He didn't address my depression though; he just smiled and told me he'd been reading my emails.

He also had me sign over custody of my youngest son, Jared, to Clog. He asked me to do that under the guise that she and her husband needed custody to get Jared enrolled in school and health insurance. "It's only temporary, until you get your health back," Jim and Lulu assured me.

Yeah, in the midst of arguing over my alleged brain damage, I signed it. After all my screw-ups over the past few years, I didn't want my kid to not be enrolled in school or not have health insurance. What kind of dad would want that? I didn't think, I signed. In my defense, I still loved and trusted Jim and Lulu.

Jim and I had flown back to Phoenix to attend my bankruptcy hearing that I missed in December during my coma. I told him I could handle going to Phoenix myself and that I would take a cab from the airport to downtown. Then I would rent a hotel room for the night, go to my hearing, and fly back the next day. I argued that would give me a chance to prove I could handle things on my own. He told me I couldn't handle it and that he was going with me. Discussion closed.

At the hearing, he handed over my $5,000 tax refund check directly to the bankruptcy judge. He never even let me touch it. My bankruptcy hearing was before the April, fifteenth deadline for filing taxes, so he didn't need to file them when I was in the hospital. He should have waited until after my hearing. But that way I would have had some financial independence. That goes against brainwashing basics. And to think when I was in the hospital I felt so reassured that he was filing my taxes for me. He knew what he was doing. I didn't know what he was doing.

I was excited to see Moxie when we were in town for my hearing, but since we were only there one night, I never had an opportunity to ask Jim to drive me to Bula's. Instead, I called her after we got back to Auschwitz. I apologized for not visiting my dog and asked, how he was doing?

"You don't need to worry about that dog. He's gone," she said flatly.

"Moxie's dead?" I asked her, stunned.

"No, I gave him away."

"You what?"

"Hey, I never asked to be a dog owner."

"You weren't," I said, my stomach in my shoes. "You gave my Moxie away? Why didn't you call me first?"

"I didn't need to call you. Look, Chris, you just need to relax and concentrate on your brain damage. Everything is being taken care of for you."

Huh?

I was devastated. "You give away my dog of twelve years without so much as calling me, and I'm supposed to relax? Everything is being taken care of for me? Holy expletive, expletive, expletive!"

I can't remember the rest of the short conversation. I realized she had given Moxie away right before Jim and I went back for the bankruptcy hearing. Aaron later suggested Father Crab must have called her and told her she better get rid of that dog or I might move back in with her. Jim had me separated from everything I held dear. The only thing left was my dog. Now he was gone too. I guess this is where he expected me to lose all remaining hope and give up. *Get back in your wheelchair!*

There are dozens more stories I could tell you about the time I spent in Texas, but I think/hope you get the gist of how things were. I was truly friendless in Auschwitz. Again, thank God for Aaron Blizzard! We talked nearly every day on the cell phone Aaron had given me back in the recovery ward. If you are reading this bro, thanks. You knew things weren't right. You told me that Jim had ill intentions for me. I told you, you were wrong. I was wrong, you were right.

I called Mom after Jim told me to console the clergy. I asked her to ask God what I should do. Should I stay in Texas or go back to Arizona? Mom said, "It sounds like you need to ask God yourself." Good advice, mom. Thanks.

# Chapter 24 Moxie Intermonial

## (Intermonial #5)

The next Intermonial I have to share with you isn't nearly as exciting as my car or motorcycle crash. It's not as odd as the bird chasing me down that country road either. I don't believe I would have even noticed it back in my drinking days. As a matter of fact, I wouldn't have sought God out in the first place if I were still boozing. But I talked to Him from Auschwitz one night and He answered me. Here is the prayer I made in the backyard one night... and the Intermonial that followed.

Dear God: I'm lost. I don't know what to do. I guess I've been lost for a while now, huh? Jim is telling me I should stay here in Texas. He tells me that he and Clog will allow me to see Jared at least once a year by either flying me to Florida or flying Jared to Texas. He says Ryan belongs in a military school for boys. He also says I'm brain damaged and can't work a job or take care of them. To me, God, none of this seems right. I think I should leave here and go back to Arizona. I feel like it's the only way I can get my life back. God, I don't know what to do. I didn't know I was going to crash my motorcycle that day. I didn't know I was going to get into a fight with Ryan and go to jail for two weeks. I know you saved me that night the ambulance showed up. Jim is wrong. Yeah, maybe I'm lucky because you did, but I know it was you who saved me. And I know you're listening to me now. That's about all I know though. God, if you tell me to stay in Texas, I will. It will go against every fiber of my being, but I'll do it if you tell me to. You know what I need. I don't. If you need me to stay here I will. I promise. I'm so lost. Please help me, God. Thanks for listening. Amen.

That was about it. I crushed out my smoke and walked back inside. Jim was sitting in his favorite chair watching the news when I walked past him to get to the bedroom I was sleeping in. Without the slightest provocation, he said (again, an exact quote minus a couple of vowels and consonants), "You ain't bringing that f****n' dog to Texas."

That one stopped me in my tracks. It had been about a week since Bula told me she gave Moxie away. I never considered asking Jim if I could bring him to Auschwitz. I wasn't happy. I didn't think Moxie would be happy there either. As a matter of fact, I even forgot Moxie in my prayer. I asked God about my boys and me. The Moxie situation just escaped my prayer. Sorry Mox.

Jim had two yappy Springer Spaniels that would have benefited tremendously from being around such a well-behaved dog as Moxie, but that would have gone against the principles of brainwashing... separate and destroy, right? If I had such an important part of my life back, I might want more. *You ain't bringing that _____ dog to Texas,* was all just part of the teardown phase.

"I wasn't going to ask you if I could bring him here!" I growled.

"Make sure you don't because it ain't gonna happen."

On another day, that would have turned into an instant fight. I would have started yelling at him and he, undoubtedly, would have started yelling back at me. I was so upset over losing my dog; that it might have even turned violent. The truth was, I didn't have it in me. I had been beaten down for so long and I was so tired, I just dropped my shoulders and went into the bedroom.

I sat on the edge of the bed and cursed his comment. Mind you, I didn't curse him, just what he said. He was still dad. But why did Dad hit me with that? "You ain't bring that f****n' dog to Texas." Wow. What did I do to deserve that, Lord?

Then it hit me. I remembered my prayer. I was prepared to stay in Texas, even though I thought it was a mistake because I was determined to prove to God I would live by His word. But God was telling me to get out of Texas. He used Jim to tell me that. I was slow (as usual) but after about ten minutes of fuming, it finally dawned on me that God had answered my prayer by having Father Jim make that comment. A skeptic could easily dismiss this one as a coincidence, but I believe Jim saying that, was an Intermonial. The next day I told him I was going back to Arizona.

Thank you, God.

# Chapter 25 Back In Arizona

## Re-re-rebuilding

Good 'ol Aaron came through for me again. Since I had filed for bankruptcy, I had no credit and no job to qualify for my apartment. He paid my security deposit and first month's rent back at Sunquench. Katie, the manager, let me move back even though I had no job or credit... bless her heart. After all the condemnation I had been through in Texas, it was reassuring to know some people still believed in me.

As for employment, I still had my dream job waiting, right? I had stayed in contact with Thurman and his son while I was in Texas and as far as I knew, things were still on hold while they awaited my triumphant return. Thurman hadn't fired Roy or his family yet since they were still waiting on me. So I thought.

I also called Bula and told her she needed to bring Moxie back or tell me whom she gave him to and I would go get him myself. Either way, I was getting the dog back.

## My Dream Job

I called Thurman on my second day back in town and told him to go ahead with his plans for changing the locks and firing Roy and his kin. *Blizzard is back!*

"Whoa," he said. "You've been gone a long time. Give me a few weeks and let me handle this my way. I'll call you when the timing is right."

Huh? After a couple more conversations like this with him, I called Richard (the typesetter who was also part of the plan) and asked him, why Thurman was dragging his feet about bringing me back to work?

"Because your foster dad called him," he said.

"Huh?"

"Yeah, when you were in Texas, Jim called and told Thurman you had brain damage. He said you couldn't possibly run a press in your condition and that all you would do is hurt yourself. Then, since they hired you back- despite being warned about your medical condition- your foster dad would have no choice but to sue Thurman for every penny he has."

Ouch.

# Ryan

Grandpa Jasper brought Ryan back to me from Michigan. Apparently, he couldn't take him a minute longer since he didn't even let him stay the two days more he needed to finish taking final exams for ninth grade. That left him Incomplete in a couple of classes. Regardless, Jasper never should have had Ryan in the first place. And I was happy to have my boy home again.

We spent the summer together and I enrolled him in tenth grade at a very nice school down the street. As a matter of fact, Ryan said of all the schools he had ever been to (about a dozen) Arcadia was the best one. He signed up for football and had a great high school career.

# <u>Jared</u>

As for Jared... I called Clog and told her I was ready for him to come home too. Jared wanted to come home and it was time for us to be a family again.

Not so fast. Remember that 'temporary' custody paper I signed so Clog and Satchel could enroll him in school and get him healthcare insurance? You know, until I got my health back? Well, *until I got my health back* were the keywords on the custody form that I didn't bother to read? I know, I know, I should have read such an important document. But I believed every one of those people was trying to help me. I didn't know about Jim closing my bank account or ruining my dream job. I didn't even blame him for doing my taxes early so he could make sure it was turned over to the bankruptcy judge to keep me from buying a car and renting an apartment for the boys and me. I certainly didn't know they never had any intention of letting Jared come home. God help me, I just signed the papers.

I called Clog after I got Ryan back and told her I was ready to get Jared home too. "You have brain damage. I'm not sending Jared back until you get another MRI... in eighteen to twenty-four months. I have to make sure he's safe."

Wow. I did not expect that. I tried to explain to her what the doctor told Aaron and how the MRI was unnecessary. "Another MRI won't show how well my brain is working even if I do wait two years to get one."

"I'm not interested in your brother's opinion. I have been discussing this with *actual* doctors and I'm going by what they told me, not what your brother thinks."

I was livid. "It's not your decision to make. He's my son and I want him back!"

"I hear anger issues. I can't hand Jared back with you sounding so unstable. Just wait and have the MRI. Then we'll talk about it again."

"YOU CAN'T KEEP MY SON!"

"Oh yes, I can. You signed the papers. I'm not going to talk to you unless you can control yourself. Just calm down."

I have to edit this part of our talk. I can tell you the conversation didn't last much longer before I hung up. If any of you are parents (or even remotely human) you can imagine how someone holding your kid would eat at your core. It set me on fire. Just reliving that on paper is tough. She refused to give me back my boy and then accused me of having anger *issues*. Wow, I had anger issues in spades.

A few days later I received a letter from her, certified mail, which I signed for. The letter opened by saying, "It's obvious you can't control yourself enough to talk on the phone so I'm writing to you instead..." It went on to say blah blah blah.

I responded with a certified letter of my own. She wouldn't sign for it and the post office brought it back. So I resent it by regular mail and sent a copy to their lawyer. Then I wrote her another letter. Then another. For the record, I didn't get a single response to any of them. Grrrr…

Speculation mode: I believe she was counting on me not writing back. I think her plan was to take her copy of the certified letter that she sent to me in front of a judge to ask him for permanent custody of Jared. Clog would argue that since I was too angry for phone conversations and wouldn't respond to regular mail, the court should grant her and Satchel Cockroach permanent guardianship over this poor, lost kid.

"Your honor, I just can't communicate with his father. Look how hard I've tried. He has anger issues and he has brain damage."

But instead, I wrote her back three letters. THREE! In one of those, I enclosed a letter from my doctor saying I didn't have brain damage. I had my regular physician check me over and write a letter stating I was in good health and that she didn't see any reason for me not to have both kids. After all, I was taking care of one. However, I'm sure those letters went straight into the trash.

# Dad (Call one)

I still wasn't angry with *Dad* though. I didn't blame him for me not getting Jared back. I blamed his daughter. I didn't even begrudge him over ruining my dream job by threatening to sue them if they hired me back. I still kept calling him every week during my first couple of months back in Phoenix. Sometimes I'd call him more than once a week. We were both with the same cell phone company so it didn't cost either of us any minutes to talk. By that point I was so used to talking to him, he's where I turned when I needed consultation.

Let me tell you about the last two conversations I had with him. That's when he changed from dad to Jim. I called him on a Saturday while working part-time for Roy. Yeah, he owned the print shop now, was unaware of our secret plan to replace him, and still brought me in to print on weekends. I was running a press alone (Yes, completely unsupervised) on a Saturday when I heard a loud explosion that literally shook the building.

I opened the back door and saw my crappy car (the one that wouldn't pass emissions) engulfed in flames. I did my level best to extinguish them with a garden hose, but within a few minutes, the fire department showed up and finished hosing it down. The bicycle I had in the back was missing and I concluded someone had stolen it and then torched my car- for kicks. Unfortunately, it had a full tank of gas.

I was twenty miles from home, with no car, no bike, and working one of my three part-time jobs. So I called Dad. I didn't call for money or help, mind you, I just needed someone to talk to. And since he was the one I was used to talking to, I called him.

At the time he was back in Michigan on vacation. Buford had rented a cabin and everyone in the family, Clog and my son Jared included, were there. I told Dad that my only ride was now a charred, smoldering mass. His reaction? He laughed. He laughed hard.

"Hold on a minute," he said. "Hey everyone, guess what happened to Chris?" Then he talked to me. "I'm sorry, I just have to tell everyone what happened," he apologized and went back to the group. "Someone blew up his car! Yuck, yuck."

Yeah, he giggled. To this day I don't remember hearing him happier. He still wasn't Jim though. That wouldn't happen until our next talk.

# Jim (Call two)

A few days later I called him again. I was working at Roy's and wanted to let him know that I had bought a used car with the little bit of money (about $1,600) I had managed to save and now I had a good running car. I was moving past my CAR-B-Q. One foot in front of the other, right? You can't keep a good man down.

"Well, we're having a blast here in Michigan! You should have come," he said, almost mockingly. Working three part-time jobs didn't leave me the money for a trip to Michigan. I had been on these trips before and they are all the same. Just like the Texas fishing trip- it is drinking from early morning to late at night, every day, all the time. And since I had just quit drinking, that didn't seem like a good environment for me to be in. Agreed? "You wouldn't believe how many cases of beer we went through the first day," he continued. "We have quite a pile of empty buildings up. I can tell you this, man." Here is another exact quote. This comment took him from dad to Jim: "Life sure is good when you got a cold beer in your hand!"

Huh?

I have told you an abbreviated version of everything... including my dissension into drinking. There are a thousand other stories of the hell I put myself through with alcohol. Jim knows a lot of them. He watched me all through high school and into adulthood. He is not a stupid man. He didn't say that comment without thinking. He is a master manipulator.

Speculation mode: I believe he said that crack about *life being good with a cold beer in your hand*, in the hopes that I would start drinking again. As far-fetched as that may sound, between him only calling me ONCE since I left Texas, and by him making that comment, he lost his right to be Dad.

# Chapter 26 Getting Jared Home

I could write a book on the ordeal I went through getting Jared home.
The entire account of backstabbing and underhandedness of what Clog
and the rest of them put me and my family through is just too painful
to relive; too long and too painful. The short version is that it took me
two years and a court-appointed attorney to get her and Satchel into a
courtroom in Florida. It also cost me every penny and all the energy I
had. All they had to do was drive to the courthouse from their home on
the golf course. Their attorney was there, but of course, they didn't
bring Jared. They wouldn't even let me take him deep sea fishing with
my brother, Tony, who is a licensed sea captain. Tony and I had to take
that trip without him. "This is not a family reunion," Clog told Jared.
Imagine.

When we did finally get to court, it wasn't even in front of a judge; it
was in front of the magistrate. I brought that letter of good health from
my doctor, but Clog argued that she had read about brain damage
(which apparently makes her an expert) and she decided a 'regular'
doctor's opinion wasn't good enough. She and Satchel (millionaires)
generously offered to pay for a specialist to evaluate my brain damage-
back in Arizona, before they could, in good conscience, release my son
back to me.

While the court was in recess, my attorney told me that if the
paperwork were forwarded to the judge this way, the judge would
wonder why I wouldn't agree to be more thoroughly examined. Having
not seen me, the judge would order us all back to court to look me over,
himself. Once again, all those two very rich people would have to do
is drive down the street. I, on the other hand, would have to take more
time off from my job and fly across the country. Finances left me no

choice but to agree to their terms.

When I got back to Arizona I scheduled a neurological exam. The result? There was no brain damage, of course. After two years, Clog and Satchel had to let Jared come home. I finally nullified that 'temporary' guardianship paper I signed in Texas. When I think about all the grief that entire cast of people put me through from the time I got out of the hospital right up until I got my son back, it makes me sick.

# Welcome Home Mr. Entitled

Jared came home with anger issues. As a matter of fact, he came home with all sorts of issues... anger only being one of them. I can't and won't discuss that, as it doesn't belong in this book. I promised him I wouldn't share his life with the world and I won't. My boys and I are best friends these days and one day they might actually read this book.

Let me just say Jared (Mr. Entitled) lived with Ryan (Pimp) and me less than six months after he came home from his two years in Florida. After several arguments, he went to live with his mother and has lived mostly with her or Bula ever since, and only seldom with me.

It seemed like he just didn't fit in anymore. He was different. He had basically gone from the projects to the penthouse... and then back to the projects. I am confident if he had stayed in Florida, he would have attended a university- instead of having one semester of community college under his belt. He was on the honor roll in Florida and he certainly responds well when being constantly supervised, monitored, and corrected. The problem was/is... he didn't have that with his family back in Arizona. His dad was a printer and his mother was a truck driver.

It is obvious, looking back, that none of the people from the Crab family ever intended for Jared to come home. Jim and Lulu would keep me from getting my life back together while Ryan lived with his grandpa in Michigan; what happened to Ryan was not their concern. They could control Jared. They thought they could control me. They thought. I don't believe they prayed.

# Chapter 27 Pastor Chris

## Pastor Chris

During my struggle to get Jared back, I decided to find a church where I could rekindle my relationship with Christ. After searching the Internet that October, I found one. I showed up for Sunday service and was greeted by Pastor Chris. We exchanged phone numbers and I sat through most of his service. For reasons I don't fully understand, I felt uncomfortable and left early. Pastor Chris called me later that day and said it was nice meeting me and that he was certain God had led me to him for a specific purpose. He told me to call him if I wanted to meet him for a private meeting before next Sunday; you know, in case there was anything spiritual I wanted to talk about.

"Okay, I'll do that," I told him; with all the polite enthusiasm I could muster, and said goodbye.

I hadn't even made it through his service, I certainly didn't want a "special" visit with him. Then I thought about Birdbrain. I thought about that ambulance showing up when I was lying on the road, next to my motorcycle, not breathing. I thought about that steering wheel ripping out of my hands the night I crashed my car at Fort Campbell. After a few hours of soul-searching, I decided that other Christians needed to hear those stories.

I was sure my divine experiences could help bring an amount, however small, of faith affirmation to others. I called back Pastor Chris and asked him if we could have that talk he offered. He said he would be delighted to meet with me. We settled on that Thursday at four o'clock, at a coffee shop down the street.

Thursday arrived and so did pastor Chris; riding his Harley, with no helmet. His showing up without a helmet on made a natural lead-in to my ambulance story. I opened by telling him about my motorcycle crash and the 'random' ambulance that saved me. When I finished, I asked him if he would allow me to tell that- and some of my other God stories, to his congregation. "I think other believers could really benefit from hearing about my experiences with God," I told him.

He opened his Bible and said, "If Christians need the truth," pointing to a random page, "they have the Bible. No offense, but you sound like a drunk who got lucky."

There was that *lucky* word again. Unlike Father Jim, he left out the f-bomb, but he was the second church leader to hear my story and just like the first, told me it wasn't God who saved me but luck. I never got to my bird or steering wheel Intermonial. I didn't even have the word Intermonial, yet.

Pastor Chris asked me how I knew I was in God's good graces if I wasn't living according to Scripture. I told him I didn't know why, but for some reason, God has always watched over me. He didn't understand how I could know that. He said unless I could stand in front of his congregation and say that Jesus Christ intervened in my life because I was following His teachings and living according to Scripture, he wasn't going to let me talk about my divine experiences. I shook his hand and thanked him for his honesty. I also told him I couldn't go back to his church.

I don't relay this story to besmirch Pastor Chris. He is a good man. He couldn't see God, however, beyond the pages of his Bible. I went home and thought about what he said and decided he was wrong. Others needed to hear my stories. Even though they're not in the Bible, they were still true. They are still affirmations that God is real and everyone needs that.

# There Really Is A Higher Power

One of the reasons Pastor Chris wouldn't let me speak at his church is that unless I could stand in front of his congregation and say this is where I was and this is how Jesus Christ brought me to this place of salvation, he couldn't see any possible advantage of letting me tell my stories. To him, they were really nothing more than a drunk getting lucky. As I said, I am a Christian. I do believe Jesus Christ is the Son of God and that is whom I fully expect to meet when the physical part of my existence ends. I honestly can't say whether it was Jesus Christ, my guardian angel, the Holy Spirit, or God Himself who has been bailing me out. But I have been seeing "God" since that van ride at Eagle Boy's.

Let me tell you one thing I know for certain: That steering wheel spun out of my hands. Let me repeat: THAT STEERING WHEEL SPUN OUT OF MY HANDS! I have gone back to that night a million times. There is simply no other explanation other than a higher power did that. Simply none.

Sure I was drunk. I was super drunk. That maneuver is not something a person attempts sober. But it happened, just the way I said it did. It was an incredible gift. Not only did God save my life, along with my passenger's lives, but also by spinning that wheel, He showed me, that He is real. He proved it to me. I believe He spun that wheel so the next day, looking at those tire tracks, I wouldn't just think I got lucky by going between that telephone pole and sinkhole. In my mind, I still see those tire tracks; six inches on either side of certain death, exactly.

# Chapter 28 Unemployment Intermonial

There are more Intermonials, but like I said, this IS an abbreviated version of my life. I didn't even get around to telling you how I became an ordained minister, about my time doing standup comedy or graduating in the Spring of 2015 from Scottsdale Community College with my AAFA in Fine Arts and Theatre. If you want to hear those stories and more details about the ones covered here, invite me to speak to your group. Pastor Chris wouldn't let me tell my stories, but maybe you will? I believe people of faith need to hear about some of the things God has done for me.

And here is one more. I'm wrapping this story up, but I promised God that if He answered my prayer, I would put this one in. Sure enough, He did. So keeping my promise, here it is. It's also a perfect example of how I see God in my daily life when I'm not crashing vehicles or being chased by birds.

## (Intermonial #6)

This one started with the last print shop I worked for, *Hotdog Press*. The short version is that the owner, *Mr. Hotdog*, decided that after twenty-three months of employment, he wanted to get rid of me. Other employees had warned me that he was famous for NOT paying unemployment benefits. Apparently, he got away with that by making any unwanted employee so miserable that they quit. Since they 'quit' and weren't 'fired', Mr. Hotdog wasn't charged extra money by the state unemployment insurance agency.

After a couple of heated arguments between him and me, he tried that tactic with me by taking me off the printing press; reducing my work schedule to two hours per day, and making me sweep and mop floors. I did this while a girl from the bindery department ran my press. I still kept coming to work though; I even mopped around her feet while she operated my machine. I understood the game Hotdog was playing. I refused to quit and didn't stop coming to work until my supervisor, Dave, told me there was no job for me. That's when I filed to collect my unemployment benefits and stopped driving clear across town to log a couple of hours of janitorial work.

I was online filling out the enrollment for unemployment benefits when I came to a part that asked me why I was no longer employed. My choices for being involuntary unemployed were either laid off or fired. They didn't have a "replaced" icon so I picked laid off. *Dog* responded by claiming that I had regrettably quit, voluntarily, during the normal Christmas slow-down that most printing businesses experience. He had a full schedule of work for me to print but I refused to come back to work.

Again, I got another book on this experience alone. I even have a plethora of smaller Intermonials of how Jesus watched over and guided me through this perilous and critical time in my life; such as my first argument with Dog that led to my unemployment in the first place. It happened THE day I was to turn in my pay stub to complete the financing on a brand new car I was purchasing. I know God didn't want me to take on five years of payments. He didn't want me to stay at that job. Here is the simplest version of my *Unemployment Intermonial*.

Basically, after reading both of the arguments we submitted, The Lady at the unemployment office concluded this matter needed to be decided by a judge. She gave us a court date, in two months. I sold my junk car- the one that I was going to trade in for a new one- and used that money ($700) along with a few loans from Brother Matt, to hunker down and begin writing this book; while looking for a job, of course.

While waiting for my appeal date to arrive and working on this story, I came up with the brilliant idea that there were people who never went to church, that still needed to hear my stories. I decided I should try to help bring them closer to God, or at least maybe make them curious. With that goal in mind, I bought the website, sinnerchurchonline.com and began dreaming up ways to make an attractive, memorable site that would attract sinners everywhere. I decided to start telling my Intermonials on video and holding regular church services that were a mix of my Intermonials along with other people's Intermonials- that they would hopefully send in.

By the time the date arrived for my unemployment appeal, I decided that as soon as I won my case- which meant getting a back-pay of two months of benefits at one time, I was going to buy a video camera and pay a graphic designer to build my website. Then I could officially launch Sinnerschurchonline.com. That was my plan. This is where the main Intermonial of this saga comes in. As I said, there were many during this ordeal, but this is a typical example of how I see God.

It was the day before my appeals hearing when I checked the mailbox and found two checks totaling over $400. That was such a wondrous and unexpected windfall when I was so broke; I should have been happy, right? Instead, my heart sank.

I knew what it meant. I understood then, just like I understand now, how God/Jesus works in my life. I had so much hope invested in my online church; to the point, that I found a website designer and drew out plans on paper; spread across my living room floor. I decided the moment I received my back pay from unemployment insurance, I was going to buy a video camera and start recording services for my online church. I was doing this for God and hoped it was what He wanted. But when I came into that unexpected money, the day before my unemployment appeal, I knew it could only mean one thing: I was going to lose in court. That $400 was God telling me that my day in court was not going to go as I hoped, but to stay in faith- He was watching over me.

The next day I found myself in front of *Judge Senile*. She was the poster child for Tenure Gone Bad. I'm sure the cerebral palsy, spinal bifida- or whatever crippling disease had disfigured that poor woman, before her last stroke, had worn her down plenty, but God bless her, she was a judge. That poor old gal had no business holding a job, let alone making legal decisions. I swear I have the worst luck with judges. Only God knows why.

Mr. Hotdog didn't have to be in court or to be in the judge's office, that day. The judge, who slurred her words so badly it was almost funny, now- almost, called Dog's office and swore him in over the phone. After his name, I don't believe a true word left his mouth. As an old friend used to say, he started *lying like a gas meter*.

Without going through all the nuances of what was said, Dog opened up by saying that I was not working many hours because we were slow- and that's why I quit. He followed that by saying he took me off the press because I was telling people that I wanted to get fired. Therefore, he was afraid that I was going to throw a wrench in, "My $20,000 piece of equipment so he would have to fire me."

I thought that simple contradiction alone was enough to prove he was being, at best, disingenuous. Then he let loose a slew of lies so egregious they often contradicted each other and were just as preposterous as his opening whopper. They were simply too numerous to follow. I didn't bring a pen and paper with me. Had I been more prepared, I could have written some of them down and did a follow-up cross-examination. But his dishonesty was so apparent, I figured why bother? He was lying to the court and playing them like fools. I was right. He was wrong. Anyone could see that, even this fragile old judge.

When it was over, the judge told me to check online later that night and her decision would be posted. I thanked her and left, thinking maybe I read too much into the unexpected money.

# Sinnerschurch OFFline

That night I went on the courthouse website and typed in my name, case number, and password; sure enough, *Judge Slur* concluded I had voluntarily quit working for Mr. Hotdog and was owed nothing. Ouch.

I was sick over the news, but not surprised. I also knew it was the end of my online church. Losing my unemployment appeal wasn't a delay or a setback in getting that site up and running; it was God telling me not to go through with my idea. Just like the unexpected money was God telling me I was going to lose my appeal, God was now telling me to give up on Sinner's Church.

For the record... I won my second appeal. A panel of, apparently sane, judges reviewed my case, listened to Hotdog's wild rant, and said the previous judge applied the wrong something when she ruled against me. I still gave up on that online church.

# Chapter 29 Why

Why me? The first time I wrote this book, I merely relayed my experiences, and quite rightly stated I had no idea why God had done these things for me. Then I read a book on writing a book and in it, the authors said people don't want a book full of questions, but rather, they want a book full of answers. That led me to literally thousands of hours of soul-searching, trying to figure out *why God has done these things in my life.* As you can see, it wasn't because I have led a good Christian lifestyle. Moxie was still with me back when I considered this question (God rest his beautiful soul) and I spent countless hours walking him, trying to figure out what makes me special.

I finally decided that what sets me apart from many other people is that I have always seen God at work in my life. In everything from that interrupting phone call to that crazy bird chasing me down the road, I have always looked for and seen God. Maybe Pastor Chris couldn't see God any further than the pages in his Bible, but I always have. After reaching that conclusion (which was a Tuesday) I went to church that Sunday to get God's take on my conclusion. The priest in attendance gave a sermon in which he read a passage, I forget, from the Bible that has since become known as my *lost verse.* After reading it, the priest said, "What this verse is telling you, is that above all other things, God wants you to see Him." After hearing him say that, I KNEW I was right. I went home, changed the book's title to Seeing God, and began rewriting it- as an answer book, not a question book.

The two most important laws in the universe: As promised here they are. Hopefully, you read this book and didn't just skip to the end. Here is my justification for each.

# #1 God is Real.

I don't say that because of the interrupting phone call. Not because of that crazy bird. Not because of that ambulance showing up when it did. Those are all evidence of God's existence, but not proof. I say that because of that steering wheel ripping out of my hands. Even if I did run over something, which I didn't- but even if I had and it made the tires suddenly turn (Twice, first left then right), the car would have rolled over. Forget executing that perfect maneuver between the telephone pole and the sinkhole with six inches to spare on either side, the car would have flipped if not for a supernatural force holding it down. Why do I say that force was God, the Father of Jesus Christ? Because that is the only God I have ever prayed to. Sure I was drunk and the only reason I know what I said is because my friends told me the next day. God, the Father of Jesus Christ, is the only God, sober or drunk, I have ever acknowledged. How do I know that is THE most important law in the universe? How do I know that is #1? Because what else in this universe could be more important than the existence of God?

# #2 God wants to be seen.

What is my evidence of that? This whole book is my evidence of that- my whole story. If you read it and didn't just skip to the end, then you know I haven't lived a God-fearing Christian life. As I said in the beginning, I am not qualified to help anyone become a better Christian. You can see from this book I haven't lived a proper Christian lifestyle. So why did God do all of the things for me that He has? Why did He send the bird? The ambulance? Why has He looked over me when I haven't even so much as asked Him to? Like I stated earlier, it's because I have always seen him, that's why.

After reading my story, can you come up with a better reason? I couldn't.

# ABOUT THE AUTHOR

Chris Blizzard is an Army veteran who, as of Spring 2015, will be a graduate of Scottsdale Community College with an AAFA in Fine Arts and Theatre. He lives with his best friend, Curly- whom he rescued on March 13, 2014. He enjoys speaking about the times he has seen God in his life and helping others see what God has done in their lives. He can be reached at Curlylovesme@gmail.com to invite him to speak to your group.

This is Curly. He is my best friend and the best dog in the world. Where I go, he goes, usually. So if you invite me to speak, don't be surprised if I ask if Curly can come with me.

# UPDATE

2017 I graduated from Arizona State University with a BA in theatre. Curly sadly crossed over the rainbow bridge on March 6, 2024. This is Maggie. I took her off the streets of Baytown, Texas, on April 12, 2024. I also adopted Cat (Not pictured); she just had six Kittens. I got myself a little family and a new home in Texas. Oh, and just like Curly, wherever I go, so does Maggie.